THE
CHORAL DIRECTOR'S
COOKBOOK

Insights and Inspired Recipes
for Beginners and Experts

Published by
Meredith Music Publications
a division of G.W. Music, Inc.
4899 Lerch Creek Ct., Galesville, MD 20765
http://www.meredithmusic.com

MEREDITH MUSIC PUBLICATIONS and its stylized double M logo are trademarks of
MEREDITH MUSIC PUBLICATIONS, a division of G.W. Music, Inc.

Cover and text design by Shawn Girsberger

International Standard Book Number: 1-57463-078-4
Library of Congress Control Number: 2006934880
Printed and bound in U.S.A.

Contents

Foreword

This choral methods and techniques book is one in a series of so-called cookbooks for music educators, the brainchild of Garwood Whaley, owner of Meredith Music Publications. The idea of collecting easy-to-find and quick-to-read ideas from experts in the field came to him Christmas 2004 as his wife eagerly flipped through a new cookbook. The cookbook series began to take shape only six months later with the release of *The Music Director's Cookbook: Creative Recipes for a Successful Program*. To me, reading the recipes was like finding trade secrets that typically remain hidden away. As a contributing author to the first book, the great value of an exclusive choral version had already occurred to me, so when asked by Gar to be the editor for this book, I had an ambitious strategy ready and waiting.

Following the pattern set by Gar in the first book, authors were asked to write about something they were passionate about in their work. In cooking terms, each recipe therefore represents a *pièce de résistance* for individual authors. Authors agreed that all royalties would go to the American Music Conference to help fund music education projects, so recipes are from the heart with the unselfish purpose of supporting and continuing the success of other choral conductors. To assure a representative variety of recipes, choral directors were invited whose success was built on outstanding records of performance, conducting, workshop clinics, recordings, research, choral composition, leadership, and teaching. Contributors to the book direct choirs of a full variety of voicings (girls', boys', women's, men's, and mixed), ages (children's, youth, high school, collegiate, and adult), sizes (small vocal ensemble to large chorus), styles (traditional, popular, and multicultural), and types (community, church, prison, educational, symphonic, and professional). You will find that some recipes provide global overviews that draw together several related issues and strategies, while others focus on specific topics in finer detail. And in the same manner that different master chefs create unique variations on a familiar recipe or mix familiar ingredients into new concoctions, in this book you will find remarkably different solutions for the same choral topic alongside new and unique topics.

Just as Mrs. Whaley so eagerly searched recipes in her new cookbook, I hope you enjoy searching the table of contents and leafing through these pages for your own favorites. Whether you use them as a quick energy snack before a rehearsal or sit down to a full course, I am sure this book will tickle your taste buds and stick to your ribs.

Alan Gumm
Editor

Acknowledgments

To each of the "chefs" who contributed to this publication, I offer my sincere thanks. All individuals responded to our initial invitation with a resounding "yes." They were all enthusiastic about being involved in what they felt would be a unique and worthwhile contribution to choral music and to music education. Their generosity has been exceptional, their expertise unquestionable, and their love of singing and music education inspiring. The writings within, presented by them, are based on years of study and experience from a variety of educational and professional levels.

Profound thanks and admiration are extended to Alan Gumm, editor and coordinator of this volume. Alan could, and should, write a book on organization and management; his skills are incredible! He is a creative and talented individual to whom I owe a great deal of thanks for his tireless work on this project. Alan went about the task of selecting authors, organizing and collecting materials, motivating writers, and editing text with energy and enthusiasm. In addition to being a superb musician, Alan is also an educator of the highest order, which is apparent in the composition of this volume. Thanks to Alan Gumm, the world now has a collection of interesting and insightful articles contained in one volume written by many of today's most outstanding choral directors and pedagogues. To Shawn Girsberger, my unending gratitude for her work with Meredith Music Publications and for the artistic layout and cover design of this volume. For leading the way in support of music education in our schools and for their assistance in marketing, thanks to Joe Lamond, President and CEO of NAMM, and Laura Johnson, Associate Executive Director of the American Music Conference. I would also like to offer my sincere appreciation to the many individuals who have encouraged me throughout my career as a writer and publisher.

And finally, to the thousands of music students and their directors who have inspired each of us, our never-ending thanks for your dedication, beautiful music making, and the belief that music does make a difference.

Garwood Whaley
President and Founder,
Meredith Music Publications

❧ ❧ ❧

My foremost thanks goes to Gar for his guidance, patience, and assurance through a year-long process from the first phone call to the final draft. Also, thanks for both the nudge and the understanding given until this project finally fit the original vision.

Thank you to each of the authors for contributions freely given. I asked for successful people, you all had the extremely busy schedules that come with being successful people, and I am grateful that you squeezed this project in somehow. It was my personal and professional joy to have shared phone, e-mail, and personal contact with folks so dedicated to lifting people up through choral music. For some, the work went beyond writing a favorite recipe—thanks especially to Steve Demorest, Ed Thompson, Hilary Apfelstadt, Pearl Shangkuan, and others whose suggestions pointed the way to other outstanding contributors to the book.

My best wishes and hope go to the American Music Conference, to which each of the authors has dedicated their royalties to help fund music education projects. This connection with AMC reveals something that is typically true of composers, researchers, and authors in this profession—it has little to do with making money and all about helping others. Thank you again, authors, and thank you AMC in your efforts to help others in music and through music.

Finally, I thank my family members—Gayle, Jordan, and Brandon—for their love and support and for putting up with the lack of attention in favor of this project.

Alan Gumm
Editor

About the Authors

Hilary Apfelstadt is professor and director of choral activities at The Ohio State University. A native of Canada, she is an active clinician and guest conductor throughout the United States, as well as Canada, England, and Cuba. The 2007–2009 national president of the American Choral Directors Association (ACDA), her ensembles have performed for regional and national conferences of Music Educators National Conference (MENC) and ACDA. She holds positions on various editorial boards and is widely published in choral music and choral education journals.

Ronald Boender is the founding conductor of Acappella Singers, which specializes in eight-part arrangements with close harmony and serves as the professional "resident singers" at Butterfly World in Coconut Creek, Florida. Their CDs are available at www.acappellasingers.com or www.butterflyworld.com. Boender also was founding conductor of the Fort Lauderdale Christian Chorale and Orchestra.

Geoffrey Boers is director of choral studies at the University of Washington (UW). His choirs have performed at national and regional conventions of ACDA, MENC, OAKE, NASM, and AMS. The UW Chamber Singers toured the Baltic countries in celebration of the founding of the UW Baltic Choral Library. Geoffrey serves nationally and internationally as a conductor, clinician, and teacher. He directs the Tacoma Symphony Chorus and conducts the Tacoma Symphony Orchestra in numerous performances each season.

Lynn M. Brinckmeyer is assistant professor of music and director of choral music education at Texas State University. The 2006–2008 national president for MENC, Brinckmeyer teaches courses in choral music education, directs University Singers, and serves as the artistic director for the Hill Country Youth Chorus.

Paul Broomhead teaches choral methods, conducting, philosophy, and research, and oversees music education at Brigham Young University and is MENC Western Division Collegiate Chair. Dr. Broomhead is a popular adjudicator and guest conductor and has given frequent presentations at state and national music and education conventions.

David L. Brunner is professor of music and director of choral activities at the University of Central Florida in Orlando. He has conducted all-state and regional honor choirs throughout the United States and is a popular clinician throughout North America and Europe. As a composer, he has received numerous ASCAP awards and the ACDA Raymond W. Brock Commission, and is published by Boosey & Hawkes. He has articles in *Choral Journal* and *Music Educators Journal*, has been on the *Choral Journal* editorial board, and is a past-president of Florida ACDA.

Simon Carrington is director of the Yale Schola Cantorum and professor of choral conducting at the Yale School of Music and Institute of Sacred Music, where he has also introduced a new graduate voice track in Oratorio, Early Music, Song, and Chamber Ensemble. Previously he was at the University of Kansas where he took the Chamber Choir to the ACDA National Convention and on tour around the world; and at the New England Conservatory where he brought the program national recognition and was selected by the students for the Krasner Teaching Excellence award. Prior to coming to the USA, Professor Carrington was a singer and creative force for 25 years with the internationally acclaimed British vocal ensemble The King's Singers.

David N. Childs serves as assistant professor of choral studies and vocal education at the Blair School of Music, Vanderbilt University, Nashville, and is music director for the Vanderbilt Opera Theater program. Dr. Childs is an active clinician and adjudicator and has conducted All-State and honor choirs in several states. With over thirty choral works in print with Santa Barbara Music Publishing and Alliance Music Publishing, his compositions frequently appear at festivals, workshops, and ACDA conventions.

Ann C. Clements is an assistant professor of music education at the Pennsylvania State University. Her areas of expertise include music participation, choral music at the middle-school level, and world music transmission, with a focus on the music of Polynesia.

John M. Cooksey is professor of music and director of choral activities at the University of Utah and one of the world's leading authorities on adolescent voice maturation. In demand as a clinician and adjudicator, including for the national ACDA convention and the International Congress of Voice Teachers, he works internationally as festival conductor, clinician, researcher, and consultant. Dr. Cooksey was awarded a Student Choice Award for excellence at the University of Utah.

Edith A. Copley is the director of choral studies at Northern Arizona University in Flagstaff. She has received a number of awards, including the Arizona Music Educator of the Year in 2004. Dr. Copley has served as an ACDA state and divisional president, presented interest sessions at various music conferences, and conducted honor choirs in the United States and international choral festivals in Japan, Germany, the Netherlands, and Tasmania.

Lynn Corbin is professor of music and coordinator of music education for the Department of Music at Valdosta State University. Her experience includes teaching choral and general music techniques, voice, and graduate courses; conducting a number of collegiate and adult ensembles, currently the Valdosta Choral Guild; performing extensively as a member of professional choirs; and serving as director of music, currently at the First United Methodist Church in Madison, Florida.

R. Paul Crabb is director of choral activities at the University of Missouri-Columbia. His ensembles have performed internationally and at state and regional conventions, and he has also conducted, studied, or taught in Russia, Austria, Hungary, England, Slovakia, Italy, and Taiwan. Crabb has been recognized with multiple teaching awards, has been published in *Update* and *Choral Journal*, and has published editions of eighteenth-century choral music with Lawson-Gould, Walton Music Corporation, Alliance Music Publications, and Plymouth Music.

James F. Daugherty is associate professor of choral/vocal pedagogy at the University of Kansas. He is editor of the International Journal of Research in Choral Singing, and serves on the editorial boards of The Journal of Research in Music Education, and Research and Issues in Music Education. Daugherty works regularly with teacher workshops and festival choirs in many areas of the United States, and has lectured and conducted in Sweden, Canada, Great Britain, and Australia.

Steven M. Demorest is chair of the music education division and an associate professor at the University of Washington. He is the author of *Building Choral Excellence: Teaching Sight-Singing in the Choral Rehearsal*, published by Oxford University Press, and the editor of a series of lectures by Weston Noble, *Creating the Special World*, published by GIA. He is the author of numerous articles on choral music and serves on the editorial boards of *Journal of Research in Music Education*, *Musicae Scientiae*, and *International Journal of Research on Choral Singing*.

Rollo A. Dilworth is director of choral activities and music education at the North Park University School of Music in Chicago, Illinois, where he was awarded the prestigious Zenos Hawkinson Award for Teaching Excellence and Campus Leadership. Dilworth's choral compositions are published with Hal Leonard, Colla Voce, and Santa Barbara Music. Dilworth is a contributing author for Hal Leonard's *Essential Elements for Choir* and the *Experiencing Choral Music* textbook series and for *Music Express!* teacher's magazine.

Dwayne Dunn is director of choral activities at Olathe East High School in Olathe, Kansas, a Kansas City suburb. Previously, he taught choral music in Texas public schools and at the University of Arizona. Dr. Dunn has guest-conducted festival ensembles in several states, has presented interest sessions and research papers at state, regional, and national music conferences, and has research articles published in *Journal of Research in Music Education*, *Update*, *Southeastern Journal of Music Education*, and *Choral Journal*.

Morna Edmundson is one of Canada's best-known choral conductors, with special interests in the areas of tone color, language, and interpretation. Her professional music career as a conductor, singer, and administrator spans some twenty-five years, including professional singer in the Vancouver Chamber Choir and director of the Youth Chamber Choir, which is part of the Coastal Sound Music Academy in Coquitlam. Morna is best known for her work as cofounder and codirector of Elektra Women's Choir, with which she has received numerous honors and awards.

Kevin Fenton is associate professor of choral conducting and ensembles at Florida State University. On ten occasions, his groups have performed at conventions of ACDA and MENC and he has conducted honor choirs in twenty-five of the United States as well as in Central Europe and China. His authored articles are in *Choral Journal*, *Music Educators Journal*, and *Bulletin for Historical Research in Music Education*.

Janet Galván is professor of choral music at Ithaca College and artistic director for the Ithaca Children's Choir. Dr. Galván has guest-conducted all-state and regional honor choirs, national honor choirs for ACDA and the Kodály Educators, and the Mormon Tabernacle Choir. She has been a headline workshop clinician in Brazil, the United Kingdom, Belgium, Canada, and at the World Symposium on Choral Music, and has served as a clinician at national, regional, and state conferences of ACDA and MENC. Dr. Galván was a member of the Grammy Award–winning Robert Shaw Festival Singers during Mr. Shaw's final years.

Mary Goetze is an innovative music educator committed to children's singing, teacher education, and multicultural music. Her synthesis of research, musical composition, and teaching practice has paved the way for children's choirs across the country. She inaugurated the ongoing Mountain Lake Colloquium for Teachers of General Music Methods and forged a new path into multicultural music education that incorporates technology and new methods for contributing to cultural understanding through music.

Stephanie Bartik Graber is director of bands and professor of music at the University of Wisconsin-Stout and conductor of the Menomonie Community Choir. Her choral and instrumental groups have toured Europe regularly since 1980, performing with community ensembles in "Communities in Concert" events. She is an active adjudicator, guest clinician, soloist, and conductor and is currently oboist with the Chippewa Valley Symphony Orchestra and the Eau Claire Chamber Orchestra.

Alan J. Gumm is a Central Michigan University music education professor and choral conductor. Career highlights include: numerous teaching awards; national and European choir tours; publication of *Music Teaching Style: Moving Beyond Tradition* and contribution to *The Music Director's Cookbook* through Meredith Music; and articles in *Choral Journal, Music Educators Journal*, and major music education research journals.

Paul D. Head is the director of choral studies at the University of Delaware, where he teaches choral literature, conducting, and methods, in addition to directing the UD Chorale and Schola Cantorum. His choirs have received much acclaim for their "ability to sing with musical commitment and expression," most recently recognized on ACDA conventions at the regional and national level. He resides in southeastern Pennsylvania with his wife and three children.

Michael D. Huff is artistic director of The Festival of Gold™ Series, operated by Heritage Festivals. A freelance pianist, conductor, arranger, and producer, he is devoted to creating circumstances in which deep, relevant learning and effective performances can occur. He spent over a decade as associate conductor and principal accompanist for the Utah Symphony Chorus, and is in demand as a clinician, adjudicator, and teacher. The work of which he and his wife are most proud is their busy home and six wonderfully engaging children.

Eric A. Johnson is director of choral activities at Northern Illinois University. His ensembles have been invited to perform at the first national NCCO conference and several ACDA and MENC conventions. Johnson has articles published in *Choral Journal* and has presented interest sessions at national and divisional ACDA conventions. He is also the artistic director for the Bach Chamber Choir and Orchestra, Rockford, Illinois and is active nationally as a guest conductor and clinician. Johnson is also President of Illinois ACDA.

Michael Jothen is professor of music, graduate program director of music education, and chairperson of music education at Towson University in Maryland. He is a nationally known music educator, choral clinician, and conductor. Michael has received many commissions for choral compositions and has been recognized by ASCAP for his contributions as a composer. He is an author of *Music and You, Share the Music*, and *Spotlight on Music* published by Macmillan/McGraw-Hill, *Experiencing Choral Music* published by Glencoe/McGraw-Hill, and *Master Strategies for Choir* published by the Hal Leonard Corporation.

Mary Kennedy taught for five years at Rutgers University and is currently an assistant professor in music education at the University of Victoria, where she teaches both undergraduate and graduate courses in addition to conducting the Philomela Women's Choir. While at Rutgers, Dr. Kennedy conducted the Voorhees Women's Choir, which toured the Pacific Northwest and Montreal and environs, and was an invited choir at Festival 500: Sharing the Voices International Choral Festival in St. John's, Newfoundland.

Henry Leck is director of choral activities at Butler University in Indianapolis and founder and artistic director of the Indianapolis Children's Choir. His choirs have performed throughout the United States, Europe, South America, Australia, and Asia. Leck has produced three videos titled *Vocal Techniques for the Young Singer, The Boy's Expanding Voice, Take the High Road*, and the recent *Creating Artistry through Movement, Dalcroze Eurhythmics* with Dr. David Frego of The Ohio State University. He is the editor of two nationally known choral series published by Hal Leonard and Colla Voce.

Diane Loomer is founder and conductor of Chor Leoni Men's Choir and cofounder and coconductor of Elektra Women's Choir, both of which have repeatedly won first prizes in national and international competitions. Her choral compositions have been published and recorded internationally, and with her husband, Dick, she established Cypress Choral Music. Diane was appointed by the University of Victoria to the University Women's Scholar Lecture Series and by Dalhousie University in Nova Scotia as Conductor Emeritus. Awards include her country's highest civilian honor, the Order of Canada, the Healey Willan award, YWCA's Vancouver's Woman of Distinction of Arts and Culture, the Queen's Golden Jubilee Medal, and Distinguished Alumni Awards.

Alan McClung, having taught secondary choral music for nineteen years, now teaches choral music education and conducts the seventy-five-voice Concert Choir at the University of North Texas in Denton. A guest clinician, guest conductor, presenter, and author, his sight-singing textbook, *Movable Tonic*, is in print with GIA Publications, Inc.

Joe Miller is director of choral activities at Westminster Choir College of Rider University. He has conducted his choirs in both national and international festivals, and has served as guest conductor for numerous honors choirs. He has served as music director at churches in Ohio and Tennessee and has performed as a solo artist throughout the Midwest and in California.

Nina Nash-Robertson is professor of music and director of choral activities at Central Michigan University. Her choirs frequently perform in regional conferences of the ACDA and MENC, and she has led student and performing groups on more than a dozen tours to Europe and China. She received her first musical training in Dublin, Ireland, where she earned awards for both singing and Irish dancing, and continues to research Irish choral music.

Weston Noble conducted the Luther College Concert Band for twenty-five years and the Nordic Choir for fifty-seven years. He has served as guest conductor for over eight hundred music festivals in all fifty states, Canada, Europe, Australia, and South America, and more than seventy-five all-state choruses, bands, and orchestras. In 1989 he was named the Outstanding Music Educator of the United States by the National Federation of High School Associations, the first recipient of this national citation. In 1999 ACDA presented him with the Robert Lawson Shaw Citation at their national convention. Weston is the recipient of honorary doctorates from Augustana College (SD), St. Olaf College, and Westminster Choir College.

Granville M. Oldham, Jr. currently resides in Los Angeles, California and conducts the Cathedral Choir at the historic Second Baptist Church. His business, GO2, is under contract with the nationally known LA's B.E.S.T. After-School Arts Program. His music management company, Voix Inspiree, has recently signed the Mendoza Twins. He also has a private voice studio and continues to appear as a workshop presenter, clinician, performer, and guest conductor.

Christopher W. Peterson is assistant professor of choral music education at the University of Wisconsin-Milwaukee, where he directs the UWM University Choir and the Men of Song. Dr. Peterson is also conductor of the Milwaukee Youth Chorale, a contributing author for the Glencoe textbook series *Experiencing Choral Music*, and a frequent choral clinician.

Rebecca R. Reames is an associate professor of music in the Crane School of Music at the State University of New York at Potsdam. Dr. Reames has guest-conducted festival ensembles in numerous states, has presented choral interest sessions at regional and national music conferences, and has papers published in *Southeastern Journal of Music Education, Choral Journal,* and *Journal of Research in Music Education.* Her college mixed choir has performed for regional MENC and ACDA conferences. Dr. Reames is a past president of the New York State ACDA Chapter.

David Riley is a retired professor from Ithaca College, where his vocal jazz ensemble received international acclaim and his teaching inspired many choral directors, jazz educators, and performers, including the internationally known New York Voices. His compositions have been featured at ACDA and MENC national, regional, and state conventions, and are published with Alfred Music, Roger Dean Productions, and Shawnee Press. Riley remains an active composer and clinician and is a summer faculty member at Villanova University.

James Rodde is the endowed professor in music and director of choral activities at Iowa State University. His noted career includes ACDA regional and national convention performances, international tours, and guest-conducting all-state choirs. He serves as the North Central ACDA Repertoire and Standards Chair for Male Choirs and is Artistic Director of the Des Moines Choral Society. Alliance, AMSI, Hal Leonard, Lawson-Gould, Mark Foster, Musica Russica, and Santa Barbara have published his choral editions and arrangements.

Kathleen Rodde is on the faculty at Iowa State University, where she conducts two women's choirs, Cantamus and Lyrica, accompanies the Iowa State Singers, and teaches choral methods and class piano. Kathleen has appeared as an accompanist and presenter at regional and national ACDA and MENC conventions, and choirs under her direction have performed at state and divisional ACDA conventions as well as the national MENC convention.

Catherine Roma is associate professor of music at Wilmington College. She is founder/artistic director of MUSE Cincinnati's Women's Choir, cofounder of the Martin Luther King Coalition Choir, and founder/director of the UMOJA Men's Choir in Warren Correctional Institution. She commissions contemporary composers, especially women, every year, and believes deeply in cross-cultural, collaborative music making. Her book *The Choral Music of Twentieth-Century Women Composers Elisabeth Lutyens, Elizabeth Maconchy and Thea Musgrave* is published by Scarecrow Press.

Paris Rutherford is Regents Professor in Jazz Studies at the University of North Texas. He directs the award-winning North Texas Jazz Singers, which has performed by invitation for IAJE, MENC, ACDA, the North Texas Jazz Festival, and is heard on thirteen professionally produced CDs. He was a member of the Dallas Symphony Orchestra (trombone) and composer/producer of music for advertising and film in Dallas, Los Angeles, and London. Rutherford is a member of the resource team for IAJE.

Joanne Rutkowski, professor and coordinator of music education programs at the Pennsylvania State University, has expertise in elementary, general, and choral music as well as music in early childhood. Her research focus is the nature of childrens' and adolescents' singing voices, and techniques and materials for helping the developing singer in a classroom setting. She has served as Eastern Division representative to the MENC National Executive Committee of the Society for Research in Music Education and liaison to the Special Research Interest Groups.

Pearl Shangkuan is professor of music at Calvin College in Grand Rapids, Michigan and chorusmaster of the Grand Rapids Symphony Orchestra. Her choirs have sung at ACDA and American Guild of Organists (AGO) conventions, and she is frequently invited as a clinician and guest conductor across Asia and the United States Dr. Shangkuan's leadership in choral music includes president of Michigan ACDA (2003–2004) and ACDA Central Division (2007–2009), and music editor of the Calvin Institute of Christian Worship Choral Series published by GIA.

Vijay Singh, professor of music at Central Washington University, has been rapidly gaining international attention for his eclectic compositions, workshops, and performances. Vijay's music is performed by educational, community, and professional groups in both choral and jazz idioms. An active bass-baritone soloist, he has performed with the Robert Shaw Chorale, Male Ensemble Northwest, and the award-winning a cappella quartet Just 4 Kicks.

Rick Stamer is coordinator of music education at Northern Arizona University. His published articles have appeared in *Update: Applications of Research in Music Education*, *Journal of Music Teacher Education*, *Music Educators Journal*, *The Southwestern Musician*, and *The Colorado Choral Director*. He has presented educational sessions at MENC national, divisional, and state conventions.

Z. Randall Stroope is the director of choral studies at Rowan University in Glassboro, New Jersey. He is artistic director of a summer music festival at Wells Cathedral (England); has conducted twenty-seven all-state choirs; annually conducts national honor choirs at Carnegie Hall, Lincoln Center, and Washington National Cathedral; has directed sixteen international tours, including China, South Africa, Japan, Finland, and Russia, and has published more than eighty choral and instrumental works. His greatest contribution, however, is his work as a teacher, and his greatest joy is watching students' faces light up in the learning process.

Barbara M. Tagg is founder and artistic director of the Syracuse Children's Chorus, conductor of the SU Women's Choir, and member of the Syracuse University music education faculty. She has presented concerts and workshops in Great Britain, Europe, Canada, Hong Kong, and China, as well as for universities and choral organizations throughout the United States. Dr. Tagg has held national leadership positions with Chorus America and ACDA.

Axel Theimer, a native Austrian and former Vienna Choir Boy, came to the United States in 1969 to teach at Saint John's University and The College of St. Benedict in MN. He is on the faculty for the VoiceCare Network, conducts Kantorei, a Minneapolis/St. Paul chamber choir, the National Catholic Youth Choir, and Amadeus Chamber Symphony. In 2004 he was inducted to the Minnesota Music Educators Association Hall of Fame. His compositions are published by Alliance Publications, Inc..

Edgar J. Thompson is emeritus professor of music at the University of Utah School of Music, where he conducted the *a cappella* choir for twenty-five years and served as chair of the department for twenty-two years. In addition to those responsibilities he was music director of the Utah Symphony Chorus for twenty-one years and served two terms as president of the Utah chapter of the American Choral Directors Association. He previously taught at California State University at Long Beach.

Robert J. Ward is associate director of choral studies at The Ohio State University, where he conducts the Men's Glee Club and the Symphonic Choir, and teaches courses in conducting and choral literature. He also directs the boychoir program for the Columbus Children's Choir. He is the editor of a children's choral music series and a men's choral series published through Santa Barbara Music Publishers.

Guy B. Webb is coordinator of choral studies at Missouri State University in Springfield. He has had an extensive career in conducting choirs at the University of Florida, State University of New York, Cortland, and New Mexico State University before beginning his tenure at what was called, until recently, Southwest Missouri State University. He has been president of the Southwestern Division of ACDA.

Susan Williamson is an assistant professor of choral music education at the University of Colorado at Boulder. In addition to twenty years of teaching choirs in public, private, and community settings, Dr. Williamson has presented and conducted for MENC, ACDA, the International Society for Music Education, and the Canadian Music Educators Association.

Judith Willoughby is the Wanda L. Bass Professor of Conducting and Choral Music Education at Oklahoma City University and artistic director of the Canterbury Academy of the Vocal Arts. She has conducted choruses of all genres in festival concerts, honor choirs, and all-state choruses throughout North America, Europe, the Caribbean, and Asia, as well as national and divisional honor choirs for ACDA. She has held leadership positions in ACDA Eastern Division, the National Endowment for the Arts, state and private arts agencies, and Chorus America, and edits a choral series published by Alliance Music.

Tom Wine is professor of music education and director of choral activities at Wichita State University. He is a frequent clinician, adjudicator, and a presenter for both state and national music education conferences. His articles have appeared in *Choral Journal*, *Contributions to Music Education*, the *Strategies for Teaching* series, and *Music Makes the Difference* text, published by MENC. Wine is past-president of Kansas ACDA. He directs the Chancel Choir at Eastminster Presbyterian Church.

John Yarrington is director of the School of Music and director of choral studies at Houston Baptist University. In addition, he directs the Chancel Choir of the First Presbyterian Church of Houston. He is author of *Somebody's Got My Robe* and *Somebody's Got My Hymnal*, and the forthcoming books *Have We Had This Conversation* and *I've Always Wanted to Dunk a Basketball*. His choral compositions are published by MorningStar, Abingdon Press, and Choristers Guild.

Steven M. Zielke is director of choral studies at Oregon State University, directs the OSU Chamber Choir, and teaches conducting and choral methods. Zielke frequently is invited to guest-conduct and present clinics throughout the United States, and has conducted performances at state, regional, and national conferences. Despite a busy schedule, he enjoys playing with his two children, gardening with his wife, fly fishing, and watching a bit of college football.

The Choral Gourmet: Music Selection and Presentation

Hilary Apfelstadt

You may be familiar with the saying, "You are what you eat." Eat junk and you will be unhealthy; eat good food and you will be healthy. A gourmet, whose passion is food, not only chooses well, but prepares and presents the food with care and attention to detail, making it pleasing to the palate and the eye. Likewise, the choral conductor whose passion is for a gourmet choral experience selects the ingredients (quality music, balanced in style), prepares them with care (completes detailed score study, leading to rehearsal ideas and conducting gestures), and presents them lovingly (rehearsing effectively and expressively, with attention to musical detail, pacing, involvement of singers, and evaluation of success).

INGREDIENTS:

High-quality repertoire (well-crafted and expressive; containing teachable content; appropriate for the ensemble)

Time and context for adequate score study; colored pencils; metronome or tempo watch; access to a keyboard for final stages; an eye for musical detail that can be communicated appropriately to the singers; a mirror for gestural practice

Rehearsal plans and teaching skills that do justice to the music and the musicians

Objective evaluation; sensitivity to the musicians' responses and progress and initiative to plan according to those

SERVES:

Singers and conductors.

Step 1. Select the music.

This is the single most important decision we make with our ensembles. Not only does the choice of music dictate the curriculum in performance-based settings; it *is* the curriculum. In addition to the criteria above (see "Ingredients"), consider: range and tessitura; text strength, content, and setting (is it a good marriage of text and music?); audience and singer appeal; curricular contribution. Ask yourself, "Can I teach and perform this with conviction?" If not, reject it.

Step 2. Arrange the music effectively.

Group the music according to musical and textual ideas. Consider the variety of keys, tempo, style, and voicing/timbre, avoiding boredom. Finally, pace the program so that it peaks in each segment.

Step 3. Study the scores.

Just as gourmet chefs select the finest ingredients, they prepare these carefully before present-ing them to their guests. So we must prepare our ingredients (repertoire). Score study is the foundation of conducting and teaching in a rehearsal. Do the following:

- **Visual scanning.** Get a sense of the "big picture." How is the music constructed?
- **Visual detail.** Now look at the details, the specific characteristics. Mark cadence points and phrasing, breaths; notice unisons and octaves as these are prime tuning spots; check chord quality for tuning and color; mark key and meter changes, as well as tempo/style changes; mark cues. (Dynamics can be marked with color: red for *mf* or more; blue for *mp* or less.)
- **Challenge inner hearing.** Sing each part; mentally listen to harmony.
- **Reinforce aurally with the keyboard as needed.**
- **Contextual study.** What is the historical setting and style? Is the editing valid?
- **Gestural transfer.** How will you show the music in your conducting?

Step 4. Prepare the rehearsal.

Having studied the score, you will be able to predict problem spots, propose solutions, and sketch out a sequential order of events. Introduce a new piece through whole-part-whole pre-sentation. Plan on an overview activity, with warm-ups selected to ready the singers, just as an appetizer prepares the palate. For example, if the piece is in a minor key, use minor warm-ups. If the piece uses crisp articulation, be sure to warm up with some non-legato singing. General warm-ups (physical stretching, breathing, mid-range phonation) should begin every rehearsal, but specific-to-repertoire warm-ups help transition to the music in a logical flow. All the ingredients of the rehearsal, as with a meal, are meant to complement each other.

Bring the musical meal to a close with a dessert or "musical moment" that provides closure and satisfaction, whether that is summarizing what you have worked on by performing it as a whole, or reviewing a familiar piece that is close to or at performance level. Reflect on the success of the meal: what went well and was received with enthusiasm? Remember your singers' responses and take those as cues. Engage them in evaluation by asking effective and open-ended questions. Then think for yourself: What was well digested? Was anything miss-ing? What "leftovers" can you use effectively in the next rehearsal? Not every meal deserves five stars but it should represent our best efforts at the time and leave the musicians wanting to come back. Rather than leaving rehearsals with a full stomach, leave with a full head and heart, nourished through satisfying musical experiences. ➤●

A Cappella Vocal Jazz in Eight-Part Harmony

Ronald Boender

Keeping on pitch in unaccompanied singing is critical, especially when pieces divide into several parts. To sing chordal harmony well, warm-ups need to build up breath control to train singers not to catch their breath and break a chord. It is a matter of getting singers used to singing fully by practicing every single week. In eight-part harmony, and especially in jazz, singers will latch on to notes that sound or feel good but are wrong notes in the chord. Holding out, or "freezing," chords across long breaths helps build necessary breath capacity, gives time to isolate correct pitches in the chord, and develops the singer's ear for rich complex chords.

INGREDIENTS:
Breath control warm-ups
Score study for difficult harmonies and chord notes
Rehearsal strategies that build breath control and an ear for harmonic part-singing

SERVES:
Choirs that sing unaccompanied, multipart harmony, especially vocal jazz.

Before the rehearsal, analyze the score and circle the chords that seem difficult to sing. Then circle specific notes in the treble clef and bass clef that are most dissonant or hard to hear in the chord. Obvious are 2nds, 6ths, 7ths, and 9ths. Jazz is full of these dense or dissonant chords.

Good breath control is lacking in almost all singers, even professionals. Almost always when singers see "soft," they will take a shallow breath. In a cappella singing, this fault is obviously exposed. Repetitive sustained warm-ups over every rehearsal will slowly make a change. So when doing warm-ups, a simple 1-3-5-3-1 on low C is fine but hold the last note for 20 seconds or more at first and keep making it longer. Go up the scale in half notes and vary the dynamics from soft to loud, working especially on the soft, remembering to make the last note sustained for at least 20 seconds.

When learning to sing difficult chords, when chord tones are really in opposition to each other, try freezing chords. Tell the singers to freeze on a particular chord in a measure, explain which notes are clashing, and have them lead into that chord a number of times, usually quite loudly so they can hear the other parts clearly.

Have the singers in the clashing notes, such as the tenor and soprano sections, face each other and sing their notes at the other section so they can hear the beautiful dissonance. Of course sometimes the beauty is not heard unless the entire chord is sung. Sometimes it takes weeks before the chords sound and sing right, so have patience while singers develop their ears for this type of harmony and chord tuning.

Every week, every month, and every year, the singers learn to see and sing the unusual style of music in vocal jazz more quickly, and it becomes easier as a director. Occasionally we even find the "right chord" in a piece that previously sounded good but was sung incorrectly, which gives everyone a good feeling of accomplishment as an ensemble. ━●

Pedagogical Pie

Geoffrey Boers

Here is a way to help ensure that your musical approach is well rounded. It assists with teaching musical awareness in the ensemble, aids creativity as the conductor tires of working on similar things over long periods, and defeats burnout, boredom, and fatigue. The recipe also helps engage students in the learning process, increases their awareness of the variety of musical issues in each selection of music, encourages application of knowledge into a broader range of topics, and builds musical skills.

INGREDIENTS:
One Pedagogical Pie Chart
Construction paper
White board and pens, or blackboard and chalk
Imagination

SERVES:
Conductor/teacher and students.

Preparation
First, enlarge and laminate the Pedagogical Pie Chart with a 2–3 feet diameter (permission to copy the chart is granted by the author and publisher). Securely mount the chart on a bulletin board through the center so the wheel can spin, with the indicator arrow mounted to the right of the wheel.

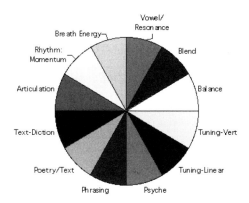

✐ *One-Slice-Per-Week Method*

Choose one of the twelve slices of pie as a focal point to your rehearsals each week for the first twelve weeks of the year. The conductor may choose a daily goal that would be applied in each piece to build to the weekly goal. For example, if the week 3 slice is articulation then the schedule would look like this:

Monday:	Introduction of terms and introduction of sounds
Tuesday:	Use of breath to create varied articulations: legato, staccato, marcato using neutral syllables
Wednesday:	Review use of breath, apply with text
Thursday:	Musical application of articulation: phrasing with legato, staccato, marcato
Friday:	Review

✐ *Leftover Pie Method*

The conductor must identify slices of the pie on which most rehearsal time is spent. Do this in two ways. First, ask the students for feedback as to which slices tend to get the most or least attention. Allow three students to go to the board to listen to the choir sing through a piece, then list the strengths of the choir and the issues that are "still cooking." Second, with a CD player, choose three varied choral recordings to listen to. As one track from each recording is played, have students write within the first minute the three most impressive qualities and the three things most in need of change. After this exercise, see if there are consistent areas that are highlighted; for instance, whether the responses were predominantly tone, phrasing, or pitch related, and note which areas are not mentioned. Once areas of attention/nonattention have been identified, develop the remaining slices of the pie using the one-slice-per-week method.

✐ *Whole Pie Method*

For this method, the conductor can keep a copy of the wheel on the music stand. First, set a goal to work on one concept, dealing with each slice of the pie in every rehearsal. Second, set a goal to draw the students' attention through questioning, demonstration, and discovery to each slice of the wheel weekly.

✐ *Pie Review Method*

After a concert, review the recording of the concert in light of the pie. Which slices are too fat and which were not served at all? Did all of the works on the concert have the same strong or weak slices? What slices need attention as new repertoire is started?

Select students in turn to go to the board. Listening to works in progress, ask each student to identify the fat, or strong, pieces of the pie, and which slices still need "cooking"? Guide the students to discover ways to focus on, rehearse, and solve problems with slices of the pie that have been undercooked.

✐ *Integrated Pie, or the Whole Enchilada*

As in the Leftover Pie Method, identify the choir's greatest strength, i.e., biggest slice. Guide the choir to discover how this greatest strength can be used to solve musical issues in every other slice of the pie. For example, our choir's greatest strength is its understanding and use of breath. How can breath energy be used to solve issues around the pie? Every slice can be used to solve problems in every other slice. Help the choir move from areas of greatest strength into areas of greatest need, as shown in the following.

Tone:	If tone is too shallow, focus on the " hook-up" of breath.
Blend:	Focus on unification of the onset of sound.
Balance:	If one section or individuals are too loud, encourage the suspension of air, rather than projection.
Pitch:	For ascending intervals, help the student imagine the space of the next pitch, then move the breath into that space ahead of the pitch.
Psyche:	Breathing together helps us feel more unified. Demonstrate and help them discover increased strength and unity.
Phrasing:	Help the choir feel the articulation, momentum, and direction of the phrase as each singer takes the breath.
Dynamics:	Help the choir feel the changing dynamics as weight or energy in the body.
Text/Articulation:	Improve cut-offs by breathing on the cut-off.
Tempo and Rhythm:	Build a sense of the physical sensation of internalized rhythm.

Does Your Verbal Feedback Nurture or Starve Your Students? Food for Thought

Lynn Brinckmeyer

Do the comments you make to students during rehearsal leave a bad taste in your mouth? Are your remarks designed to positively reinforce or punish? Unfortunately our verbal messages sometimes bring out the exact behaviors we are hoping to extinguish. Music teachers are notorious for seeking out small inaccuracies that exist in a single measure. Why then, is it so unusual for us to offer positive observations that are as detailed and explicit? Too often when choirs sing the correct rhythms and pitches musically, with perfect tone and dynamics, we give them global feedback. We simply congratulate them by saying, "Good!" Or worse, when things are good, sometimes we say nothing at all.

INGREDIENTS:
Choral ensemble
Director with a desire to improve
Accompanist (optional)

SERVES:
All choral music teachers and students.

As directors, we are here to serve students and create a musical experience that is only possible by working with other human beings. Dealing with people is not a choice in our job. However, we do choose how complicated to make that process by setting our priorities. You must decide which is most important to you, process or product. That decision will affect how you teach, the things you say, and how much your students learn. Is the final performance the highest priority or are you willing to take precious rehearsal time in order to foster a quest for lifelong learning? Example: The process of teaching sight-reading skills is time consuming at first, but eventually your students learn music at a much faster pace.

Do you continually begin your instructions with *I want, I need*, or *I'd like*? Consider how your choristers perceive that relentless message. Instead, try using student directives. Rather than saying, "I need you to stand up straight and look at me," say, "Feet on the floor, eyes front" or "Chin level with the floor." Also, refrain from judgment statements such as, "You shouldn't be mad," "You shouldn't think that," or "You shouldn't feel that way." Allow your students to hold differing views and guide them in appropriate ways to express their thoughts respectfully.

Precisely describe the behaviors you are observing. Phrases such as "all eyes are on the conductor" and "shoulders are low and relaxed" provide helpful information for your singers.

Be as accurate and detailed in providing your positive reinforcement as you are in describing the errors in their singing. You might jot down a few specific, reinforcing phrases to use with your choirs until this type of feedback becomes automatic for you.

If our students enjoy and value their experience in the classroom, learning will occur. Consistent negative messages from the conductor foster an environment that is less open to learning. If your delivery comes across as aggressive, students in your ensemble may be so distracted by your manner of speaking that they no longer attempt to comprehend the meaning of your words. Take notice of the number of negative words that fly out of your mouth such as *stop, don't, shh, can't, not, shouldn't,* or *won't.* Balance these with constructive statements. Better yet, rephrase your words to convey the same idea in an optimistic way. However, be sure to remain professional and confident. Does your habitual vocabulary include repetitive words or phrases such as *okay, alright, you know, you guys,* and *uhm?* Singers in your ensemble may become so preoccupied by these that they miss your intended communication.

Remember that each of us acquires information through auditory, visual, and kinesthetic processing (assuming there are no physical challenges such as a hearing loss). Verbal feedback may work for some of your students, while others might need additional kinesthetic experiences or visual aids to grasp concepts. Listen—really listen. In the same way that we expect students to listen critically and analyze their own singing in rehearsals, it is also our responsibility to listen to our own contributions to the classroom environment.

Provide opportunities for students to manipulate their language skills. Singing in a choral ensemble provides an excellent vehicle for this. Furthermore, with your model as a guide, singers can analyze their performances and learn to generate their own detailed, appropriate feedback to other members of the choir. When questions are employed instead of lectures, the responsibility for learning and problem solving is shifted back to the choir members. Examples: *What do you have to do as a responsible musician to create a more gradual crescendo? Who should emphasize their vocal line to be most prominent at letter A? Which section is listening to their vowels?*

Assess the type of environment you create with your reinforcement or criticism. Record (video or audio) your rehearsals to monitor your routine speech patterns. Would your students say they are starving for nurturing feedback? Dr. Peter Boonshaft reminds us in his book *Teaching Music With Passion* (Meredith Music Publications, 2002) that students will probably not remember missing an accidental in rehearsals but will remember how they felt performing in ensembles. Our goal is to serve students and to guide them on a musical journey. By examining how we impart information to the singers in our choirs, we help build a community that is essential for creating meaningful, musical memories. ➟

Increased Individual Learning in the Ensemble Setting through Problem Solving

Paul Broomhead

Think of all of the problems to be solved in order to make great choral music. How do you produce a sound that is both warm and resonant? How do you maintain your individual richness of tone while blending with singers around you? How do you create tone energy while singing softly, or sing a descending line in tune, or rectify syllabic stress/release with melodic and rhythmic emphasis? Learning how to deal with these and countless other musical problems might be considered the substance of a music education. But in some ensembles, conductors do nearly all of the problem solving and students merely follow instructions. This recipe addresses the importance of students' engagement in problem solving during their precious time with music teachers.

INGREDIENTS:
Problem-solving opportunity and responsibility

SERVES:
Since problem solving is a key way of learning, this recipe is particularly important in public school settings where the education of the individual student is the teacher's civil duty. However, this recipe really is also appropriate for choirs of every level and type. Students are able to begin solving choral problems as soon as they are old enough to be in a choir, and they do not outgrow it even at the highest levels of choral performance, so long as student learning is a priority.

Opportunity: How can we provide opportunities for student problem solving in a setting where the expectation is that the leader solves the problems and the students follow?

For each rehearsal, plan a problem-solving opportunity that corresponds with whatever principle or skill is being emphasized that day. For example, if phrase shaping is a skill you want students to learn, reserve a few phrases from each piece for student problem solving. Refrain from revealing your interpretations during those phrases (through conducting or otherwise). Then, when phrase shaping comes up as the area of emphasis, give students the opportunity to make shaping decisions, both from among the phrases you reserved for this purpose and from outside the performance literature. This does not replace verbal instruction regarding how to use syllabic, melodic, and rhythmic information to make shaping decisions. Instead, it should accompany the instruction in the same way that working out math problems for oneself accompanies the teachers' chalkboard explanations.

Here are some ways you can encourage problem solving:

"Take 30 seconds and decide how to shape this phrase." "Let's hear it. Remember, stay true to your own decisions." "Wow, I heard some great ideas. The most prominent was something like this . . ." "Do it again and I'll conduct this time and unite our interpretations." "You folks are really becoming musical artists. Nice stuff."

Responsibility: How can we engage individuals in problem solving in a setting (ensemble) that makes it so easy to rely on others and simply follow?

As problems come up in rehearsal, refrain from immediately solving all of them. Frequently assign students, as a class or in small groups, to provide the solutions. If these instances become regular and expected, learning will accelerate as students' level of mental engagement in the problems becomes automatic.

Make sure that your procedures cultivate individual accountability. Even when a task is given to the entire class, each individual must be responsible for some kind of response, such as giving an answer on cue, performing some motion representing a chosen solution, or standing on their chair when a solution is ready.

"Stand up as soon as you think of one thing you will change in order to improve intonation in this spot." "On my cue, tell me in two or three words what you have decided to do." (cue) "I think I heard 'more energy,' 'spin the tone,' and 'descending lines.'" "Now raise your hand and give me three more answers that I didn't say." "Great, now *do* what you said." "Wow! That improved a lot. Now let's all focus on singing with more energy and watching the descending lines."

It's All in the Ingredients: Considerations for Choosing Repertoire

David L. Brunner

Selecting repertoire for a well-rounded choral curriculum is a conscious process that is a lot like shopping for ingredients for a successful dinner party. The care I take in selecting my ingredients and the quality of those ingredients determines the outcome and success of my cooking experience, the nutritional value of my meal, and the ultimate enjoyment for my guests and myself. The richness of the repertoire our choral students sing is the basis for the quality of experience they will have. The repertoire is the curriculum that influences our understanding of different times and cultures, the singers' growth in understanding and skill development, and the audience's education and enjoyment.

INGREDIENTS:
Quality literature of many tastes

SERVES:
All chefs *de choeur.*

As teachers, we search for music of quality and integrity that connects with something inside of us by its elegance, craftsmanship, honesty, or beauty—music that has something to say. The repertoire provides a vehicle for shared emotional knowing: of wonderment, conviction, playfulness, thanksgiving, and every other emotion known to us all. It also provides a means for connecting with an orderliness that brings similar fleeting structure to our own lives—a reflection of our lives in minutes of sound.

A diversity of musical material broadens our exposure to different sounds, styles of singing, cultures, and traditions, and gives us an expanded understanding about what is beautiful, expressive, meaningful, and possible. A diverse curriculum consists of music of many styles, languages, challenges, traditions, and contexts. It provides the basis for building vocal and aural skills, musical thinking ability, and aesthetic awareness. Acquisition of the technical skills necessary to understand and perform a piece of music enables students to unlock the meaning of the words and experience expressive and emotional knowing.

When shopping for the right ingredients, critically evaluate repertoire for its value with regard to both teaching potential and expressive qualities. This involves practical, artistic, and personal considerations.

Practical considerations are those that are specific to a choir at a given time. Knowledge of our singers' vocal development influences the choice of repertoire with regard to age-appropriate ranges and tessituras, text, and musical challenge. These considerations vary, based upon the singers' chronological and emotional age, musical background, and vocal experience. Choose repertoire that stimulates musical growth. The music should be appropriately challenging: not too easy so that singers are bored, but neither too difficult that they become frustrated.

Artistic considerations have to do with those elements that contribute to learning and that produce an artistic effect: how well the piece is crafted, its voice-leading, text-setting, form and architecture. Choose music that is vocally conceived and that enhances the natural flow and inflection of the words. Look for pieces from which you can teach musical concepts and vocal skills.

Personal considerations are those we bring to the selection process. Are we limited in any way by our aural, keyboard, language, analytical, or rehearsal skills? Our biases or inadequacies should never limit the selection of repertoire.

The ability to evaluate repertoire requires taste and judgment, which is acquired through exposure, experience, and understanding. Our fullest understanding comes from an immersion in musical thinking and doing: an intimate interaction with a piece through study and analysis, singing and problem solving, then devising appropriate rehearsal strategies for student success.

The selection of literature is the critical factor in the consistent development of healthy vocal singing, expressive performance, musical learning, and emotional knowing. How fortunate that, more than ever, the whole round world of choral music is available to us. The Western classical tradition comprises a small part of the world's music. Be open to the wide diversity of musics and choose beyond your personal preference and experience. Make each piece a deliberate and reasoned choice. It's all in the ingredients.

Tasting the Text: The Missing Ingredient

Simon Carrington

All choral chefs agree that standard recipes should contain blend, balance, reliable intonation, voices produced in an acceptable manner, and a reasonable range of dynamics. Unfortunately for our palates the importance of the key ingredient, the text, is too often overlooked! We have the unique privilege of singing words and tasting the text. Let's enjoy the flavors! Many of our finest voice chefs emphasize the fat content—the throat space, the position of larynx, the raising of the palate—but let's also give attention to the herbs and spices, the delicate organs of communication.

INGREDIENTS:
Mouth, lips, tip of the tongue, eyes, teeth, forehead, cheekbones, and, tastiest of all, the ears

SERVES:
Choirs of all sizes.

Essential Techniques
First, study the structure of every sentence, in whatever language, in whatever period of music. Consider the significance of nouns and verbs against prepositions and conjunctions. Consider the importance of individual adjectives and adverbs and their poetic significance. Have everyone mark the points of emphasis in the score.

Second, consider the weight required on every syllable: some of the clumsiest word stresses are often found in English! To emphasize this point, have the diners savor their names with the stresses on the wrong syllables: siMON carringTON, CONnectiCUT, or some local delicacy from your area.

Third, sing an English text as it would be spoken by a good reader without any curious "singer's" vowels, sprinkle IPA (International Phonetic Alphabet) delicately on the mix, but don't overdo it! Read the text aloud, question the stress and flow, dwell on the more powerful words, pass over the weaker. Don't be afraid of diphthongs, which are such an expressive ingredient in English and German choral recipes, for instance. Relish and extend the softer liquid consonants: *m, n, l, ll, w, v*. Let the double consonants linger on the tongue: *ng, nt, nd, mp*—the possibilities are endless. However, spare the ubiquitous and intrusive *s* and *t*.

Finishing Touches: Use the Power of Imagination to Color the Text
Consider the meaning of the emotive words and how best to depict them in sound. Guide your singers to vary the vocal color of your choral dish. Have them sing certain significant

chords using different tone qualities: *soft, hard; warm, cold; dark, bright; rich, thin; sumptuous, meager*—to suggest just a few. Ask singers to imagine their voices at different stages of their lives, to sing with an appropriate tone to reveal the palette of colors available, to think of vibrato as an expressive device instead of a choral problem. Guide them as to when to sing with no vibrato, with a little vibrato, or with considerable vibrato, and when to sing with edge, with warmth, and how to vary the degree of air in the tone. With the text as your guide—ask for a bright focus, a medium-body sound, or a heavy chest tone; add special ingredients such as a more nasal quality, a heady quality, or a reedy quality, to taste.

Vary your mixture both to reflect the obvious and to suggest the hidden meanings in the text. Seasonings could include *inner calm, reflection, commitment, intensity, drama, tragedy, melancholy, joy, passion, resignation*—the range of possibilities is endless.

Chefs should feel free to add their own ingredients to taste but, above all, strive to avoid anything too bland. Remember, from *blend* to *bland*—just a short walk downhill! ➤

Putting the Zest Back into Intonation: Alternatives to Simmering or Stewing in the Choral Rehearsal

David N. Childs

Intonation is critical to developing an exciting, exquisite performance, which can literally be a metaphysical experience if all the fundamental pitches are pure and perfectly tuned, and the upper partials are activated. Be consistent with your ensemble and never accept poor intonation. If out-of-tune singing is ignored, this may become habitual. The problem will only be exacerbated in subsequent rehearsals.

INGREDIENTS:
One dollop of passionate singers, a dash of accompaniment, a pinch of direction, and a dusting of fine repertoire. Blend all ingredients together, allow to ferment, mold to taste. Net weight: a choral gastronomy!

SERVES:
All choral and vocal students, choral directors, and educators.

There is no single factor leading to flat or sharp singing. Therefore, different solutions are needed to address different factors.

Select appropriate **literature**. Choral pieces that are too "big" and that place too great a demand on young voices dynamically or in duration will lead to vocal fatigue that affects intonation. The dynamic range of young voices is not as great as their mature counterparts. If a work calls for a *ppp*, accept a *p* or even *mp*. Conversely, if a middle school choir is asked to sing *ff*, a resultant rehearsal and performance dynamic of *mf* is sometimes more realistic.

Careful **rehearsal pacing** of the repertoire can help spare the singers from fatigue that affects intonation. For instance, place pieces with a high tessitura toward the beginning of rehearsal, separated with one or two pieces with lower tessituras.

Warm up the choir for at least five minutes before each rehearsal. Work both the lowest and highest registers. Instruct the basses to continue into their falsetto range once out of their modal voice.

Dispense with the piano as much as possible. Encouraging independence in your choir will empower your singers, who will ultimately be more proactive about improving intonation.

Encourage good **posture,** excellent **breath support,** and good **vocal technique.** Frequently remind your singers to keep the rib cage expanded and the shoulders down. Model good posture when conducting. Consider having the choir stand for more of the rehearsal. An unsupported sound placed too far back in the throat has a tendency to flatten; a pushed, bright, and tightly produced sound (common in soprano voices) will sharpen the pitch. Too much pressure or muscle tension in the breathing apparatus may result in sharpening of pitch. Every so often, have your choir members massage their faces, necks, and temples, then have them tongue-trill ascending and descending triads to free up the tone. Tongue trilling, or lip trilling for those who find the former physically impossible, encourages a relaxed vocal production. A lighter, well-produced sound is much more likely to produce good intonation as opposed to a heavy, darker, cultivated quality.

Encourage uniformity of **vowel formation**. Agreeable, purely formed vowels in an ensemble help with the production of accurate intonation. Have the singers breathe through the vowel when singing onsets.

On voiced **consonants** (such as *v*, *b*, and *m*), have singers hum the pitch softly for a microsecond before they begin full-voice singing, imperceptibly so that the singers are not actually heard. This can encourage singers to find their own pitch before phonating with the choir.

Explain to your choir the **physics of sound**. If singers know what to listen for in a perfectly tuned chord, they are apt to seek it out more often. Experiment with unisons, octaves and perfect fifth intervals on a bright "*ee*" [i] sound and have them listen for overtones. Encourage your singers to match the frequency (pitch) and amplitude (volume) of their neighbors. It is difficult to impossible to tune to others if choristers cannot hear the product of their own voice. Have them sing microtones on any vowel, always returning to the original pitch upon your command. Ensure that the lowest "fundamental" choral voice part—bass in mixed or male choirs and alto in treble choirs—is strong and in tune. Failure to tune the lowest voice part will result in out-of-tune singing in upper parts, and subsequently in the entire ensemble, no matter how strong the upper voices are.

Analyze the music for **pitch direction** and **intervals**. Descending conjunct passages will want to flatten, especially in the male voices. Ascending conjunct phrases will have a tendency to sharpen. Have choir members imagine they are climbing or stepping up stairs when singing a downward scale or phrase; have the sopranos imagine themselves stepping downward when singing an ascending phrase.

Determine the **scale degrees** that present intonation problems. Typically the second and fourth degrees of a scale are never as high as they should be, particularly in a descending passage; the leading tones are also usually lower than they should be; the third degree in a major key or chord are traditionally higher than they need to be; and there is a tendency among young singers to leap too far below a pitch when singing larger descending intervals of a disjunct nature, and conversely a tendency to sing under pitch on upward-leaping intervals. When singing leaping passages that return to a common note, have the singers silently think that note when leaping away from it so that it is of the same height it was when they originally sang it. This term is sometimes known as **placement**.

Teach your students solfège. There are those who argue in favor of fixed-*Do* to help with intonation, but this can prove a little impractical if it is not taught intensively or from a very early age. In cases where time constraints are a factor, the teaching of movable-*Do* is certainly better than no system at all.

Encourage the singers to look ahead musically to consider the entire phrase rather than singing intervallically note-to-note. One can develop a better overall sense of intonation just as one can develop a holistic sense of form or synopsis.

Give long, sustained pitches special treatment. These have a tendency to flatten and they require good breath control. Have your choir/section stagger the breathing in such sections. Repeated notes will likewise flatten unless the singer is encouraged to mentally think each one a little higher than the previous note.

Change the performance **key** of a piece. Some pieces sit uncomfortably in the so-called break or passaggio of particular voice parts, especially young tenors. Shifting up or down a half step can alleviate the vocal discomfort that affects intonation. In general, try to avoid singing in F major and its relative D minor when possible.

Allow yourself and the choir ample time to rehearse and adjust to the **acoustics** of each performance venue. Reverberant, warmer acoustical environments generally aid in the production of good intonation as there is usually a greater fold-back of sound. However in overly reverberant acoustics, too much of an echo may result in sharpening of pitch. In very acoustically dry environments, singers can find themselves in a void of sorts, finding it difficult to hear across the choir and to subsequently tune to the other singers. In such instances experiment with the formation of your singers, have the ends of the lines more curved inward, and place singers closer together.

Scrambled eggs? Have the choir sing in mixed SATBSATB **formation**—also known as quartets, scrambled, or fruit salad—to encourage students to tune to the other voice parts more attentively.

Change the **weather**. Anecdotally, days during which there is an atmospheric change in pressure, or days that are hot, humid, and muggy, appear to affect the intonation of your choir. In addition, your students are likely to be physically and mentally unmotivated and they are more likely to sing out of tune. Call your local meteorologist and complain

Have your choir **relax** and have some down time or quiet time immediately before a concert. Too much anxiety or excitement can adversely affect pitch. Have a "no talking for 15 minutes" policy where students sit, walk, lie down, massage, or meditate before presenting a concert. Having such down time is often better than last minute run-throughs or repairs. ➝

Invitation Etiquette: The Do's of Building Choral Participation

Ann C. Clements

Building choral participation is an important skill for all directors, whether they are working within a developing or well-established program. Directors play a key role in developing their choirs, which requires them to balance their desire for increased membership with their personal philosophy of teaching and directing. In order to balance these issues, directors need to have a clear idea of where their program is heading and knowledge of the ways in which they can attract the kinds of members that fit the philosophical and performance goals of their program. The ability to recruit new members necessitates a specific kind of etiquette that goes beyond a simple invitation.

INGREDIENTS:
A solid philosophy of teaching and directing
A clear understanding of administrative and performance goals
A plan for the long-range participation goals of your program
The willingness to find creative ways of seeking potential members

SERVES:
Potential choir members.

Important Considerations: Defining Your Current Program
Growth of a program begins with defining the current program. Start this process with an evaluation of the expectations that you and others have for your program. How would you define the current state of your program: new, developing, established, or well established? What are the musical expectations for your program? Is participation for all stressed or are you seeking a high level of musical performance? As it is more than likely that your program has expectations that are not set solely by the director, take into consideration the administrative expectations for your program. If you are teaching in a school setting, make sure that you know the growth expectations of your school administration. How many students would administration like to see involved? If you are working with a community ensemble, attempt to determine the expectations of your potential audience members. What kind of choir are audience members expecting to see in a performance setting?

The second step in the process is to ensure that your expectations for growth *match* those of administration and others. Keep in mind that you are the choral expert and ultimately it is your responsibility to create a program that best meets the needs of choral members. Make sure that you have open communication with others about your ideal directing situation and choral program. If there are differences in expectations, seek ways in which to compromise without affecting the overarching teaching and philosophical goals of your program.

Plan Ahead: Managing the Growth of Your Program

In order to increase your membership and create the ideal teaching and directing situation, you must have a long-range plan for growth. Growth can happen quickly or more moderately, and there are advantages and disadvantages to both.

A quickly growing program allows for immediate change. For programs where the pressure is on to increase numbers, a plan for a quick boost to membership may appear ideal. In new or developing programs, an immediate increase in numbers may allow you to work on more complex literature, increase the number of voice parts you are able to perform, or add additional performance opportunities to the calendar. However, a rapid growth in membership also has its disadvantages. When all-calls are posted, you may be attracting new members who have different visions of choral singing than you do, or may have additional nonmusical reasons for joining choir. Keep in mind that these members may end up costing you more time or frustration than their membership is worth.

If time allows for a more moderate growth in membership, you may end up with members who truly fit your musical expectations and philosophical goals. Although a moderate plan for growth may not get the initial positive feedback from administration or potential audience members, it does allow you time to be thoughtful in the ways in which you attract potential members, eventually leading to new membership that falls in line with your teaching and directing goals. The key here is to continue communication with administration. With either plan for growth, make sure that administration and audience members know that there is a plan of action; be able to explain why you have chosen that plan.

The Guest List: Finding New Participants

Finding new participants takes creativity and a willingness to experiment. In all settings, make sure that people know you are looking for new members. Post fliers, make announcements, hold informational meetings, get names of potential members from your current members, allow potential members to sit in on a rehearsal, advertise your performances, and send personalized letters of invitation. As nothing breeds success like success, choose literature that is appropriate for the current level of your singers and ensure that they are well prepared for performances.

For those working in school settings, speak to guidance counselors or those responsible for facilitating student schedules about your desire for new members. Ask classroom teachers or music teachers in schools that feed into your school for a list of students who may be potential choir members. Attend the choir concerts of feeder schools and address choir members personally. Plan out-of-class musical and nonmusical activities that highlight the unity of your current choir program. Attend athletic events en masse. Purchase choir t-shirts that will serve as walking advertisements for your program. When your choir is confident and able, volunteer to sing for school assemblies. Ensure that all choir events are well advertised. Congratulate choir members on their achievements during school announcements. Involve parents in as many choral activities as possible, as they are a great form of communication with other community members. Use your "musical ears" when outside the classroom to find students in the halls, cafeteria, and athletic field who appear to have distinctive voices or who speak in difficult-to-find vocal ranges.

For those working with community ensembles, advertise in print or on the radio. Often nonprofit organizations can advertise for free or at a reduced cost. Have your members seek out singers and ask them to communicate directly with these potential members. Create new performance opportunities for your ensemble that may include different kinds of performance venues and that may attract a different audience. Consider expanding the repertoire or genre of music performed for a single concert or concert series, as this may attract potential members who are interested in a specific style of music. Often their musical interests can be expanded once they join an ensemble.

"Don'ts" to Avoid—What Not to Do

- ☑ Don't compromise the quality of your teaching, directing, or ensemble to grow in numbers.
- ☑ Don't cast your net too shallow or too far. Some of your best singers may come from unexpected places, while sometimes a net thrown too far will attract those who are not truly in line with your goals and philosophy.
- ☑ Don't sacrifice planning time or your relationship with current members in order to attract new members. �‒●

Kinesthetics and Movement in the Choral Rehearsal

John M. Cooksey

Kinesthetics can be thought of as the body's response to music. Movement is an essential part of the whole person's response to choral singing. Kinesthetics can be a right-brain "felt" experience in which the body feels the process of performing music. It can also be a left-brain experience of analytical thinking, in which the singer conceptualizes, analyzes, and develops perceptual awareness of the "felt" experience. Therefore, kinesthetic movement activity in vocal warm-ups and the choral rehearsal itself can encourage efficient and creative body/mind responses to music.

INGREDIENTS:
Stretching exercises
Body relaxation activities
Bending
Brain/body coordination
Facial warm-ups
Gesture and full body movement, including hand and upper body gestures, arm movements, and hand gestures

SERVES:
All choirs, all ages, and ability levels.

There are two primary areas or situations where kinesthetic movement activities can be balanced and applied: 1) vocalises and physical activities, and 2) the choral rehearsal itself. The first five ingredients listed above are excellent for use during the warm-up time and can be utilized in any combination.

Stretching exercises. These might be explored first by reaching up slowly, one arm first, then the other, and stretching. Stretch both arms and stand on the balls of the feet to balance the whole body. Gradually allow the arms to come down at right angles to the body while simultaneously bringing the heel down to a normal position. Another example would be to place the left arm over the area above the elbow of the right arm, and gently stretch or pull using the left arm. Try the reverse for the right arm.

Body relaxation. There are many body relaxation activities. Close the eyes and do deep breathing. Shake arms and legs in different combinations. Explore hand-patting exercises beginning on the lower leg and coming across the abdomen and going down the other leg.

Bending. Bending exercises should be coordinated with breathing inhalation and exhalation exercises. You might bend forward and check where you bend–from the hip or the back. Make sure the head "hangs" and is not locked in place. Gradually return to the normal position. One might exhale when first bending and exhale when returning to normal standing position.

Brain/body coordination can include touching the left knee in sequence to a moderate beat. Hand jives, in which students follow a pattern of hand clapping and finger snapping by the conductor, are also wonderful for developing brain/body coordination.

Facial warm-ups include massaging the temple, cheeks, jaw, neck, tongue base, etc. Also one can have singers imitate with the face objects such as a prune or watermelon, or spread wide in east/west directions.

Gestures and full body movement–including hand and upper body gestures, arm movements, and hand gestures–are appropriate for both vocalises and rehearsal singing. These movements can enhance creative and efficient body responses to music and directly reflect the style and expressive aspects of the score/vocalise. Choral singers will discover many ways of physically moving with music. If approached wisely, they will not develop a dependency on these movements, but instead will internalize the physical and emotional responses creatively applied. The following examples might be applied in a number of ways.

- Pulsing with light hand movements on the leg to encourage a sense of rhythm and tempo.
- Smooth horizontal movements for expressive phrasing and legato singing.
- Vertical staccato beat gestures to produce lightness in the tone and rhythmic precision.
- Arm gestures to show the rise and fall of intensity in the musical phrase.
- Full-body light walking in place to the pulse of the music, which helps to internalize rhythmic and tempo accuracy.
- Conducting the beat pattern, which is easy for students to learn and helps them to be creative; request that their pattern reflect the style of the music.
- Knee bends at the tops of arpeggios, which helps eliminate throat tension.
- Pulling motion of the arm to achieve various levels of intensity.
- Sidestep (body moves to the pulse) movement to spirituals, if appropriate.
- Arm motions going in opposite directions from ascending and descending pitches to promote relaxation responses and more efficient scalar tone.

Kinesthetic exercises are wonderfully effective when working for efficient tone and expressive singing. The ideas presented are just a beginning towards developing a varied repertoire of movement activities in the choral singing experience.

Read More About It

Cooksey, J. M. *Working with Adolescent Voices.* St. Louis, Missouri: Concordia Publishing House, 1999.

Dickson, J.H. "The Training of Conductors through the Methodology of Kinesthetics." *Choral Journal*, March (1992): 5-20. �➤

Diction al Dente: Preparing Texts "To Taste"

Edith A. Copley

The text is an important aspect of choral music containing a number of ingredients. Unified diction is a colorful entree that is "good for you." It contributes to the overall quality of the sound, improves intonation, and takes singers beyond the music.

INGREDIENTS:
Vowels
Consonants
Syllables
Words
Phrases

SERVES:
All choirs.

STEP 1. Gently crack apart each word and separate the vowels from the consonants; pronounce all the sounds of each word aloud.
Pronouncing every sound found in each word identifies the vowels and consonants that may or may not need special attention. When each sound is sung precisely the same way and at the same time, the text is much more likely to be heard and understood.

STEP 2. Roll out the vowel. (This is not a polka song.)
Vowels carry the tone, so they must be sung as long as possible. Select an initial voiced consonant connected to various vowel sounds, then ask the singers to shape and sustain each vowel as they "paint the house" (*á la Karate Kid*), using a side-to-side motion with their hand. The initial consonant should change quickly with each new brush stroke. This technique helps singers to see, hear, and feel sustained vowels.

STEP 3. Place vowels in the right container.
Some vowels are open [a], and some vowels are closed [i], however, all vowels are produced with the same sense of "inside space." Too much drop in the jaw ("outside space") reduces the space in the pharynx, which interferes with vowel integrity and lessens the "ring" in the tone. Ask singers to gently put their fingertips together at waist level, then slowly pull their hands apart on the inhalation. On the onset of the vowel phonation, they should touch their fingertips together gently, then immediately lift the right hand up toward the right ear while slowly lowering the left hand. This exercise helps singers take a diaphragmatic breath, coor-

dinate the onset, and visualize "inside space." When "inside space" is coupled with proper forward placement, it produces efficient and resonant tone.

STEP 4. Experiment with color and then brush it on each vowel sound.
The human voice is capable of singing a variety of colors from light to dark. Seek and find repertoire that gives singers the opportunity to experiment with the large palette of vocal color that is available to them.

STEP 5. Gently tap in vowel uniformity.
Unified vowels can be greatly enhanced by rhythm. To achieve better rhythmic precision, ask each singer to lightly tap subdivisions of each beat on their sternums as they sing. Instruct the singers to consistently place the vowels *on the beat*. This technique helps to unify the vowel, because everyone arrives on the same vowel at the same time.

STEP 6. Thinly slice consonants, add a little spice, and rhythmically place them in each vocal line.
Consonants clarify the message and keep the chorus rhythmically together. As a result, consonants must be sung quickly and *ahead of the beat*. Sung consonants need more air moving through them than spoken consonants. Ask the choir to whisper the text. This technique requires even more air passing through the consonants than singing the text. Keep the consonants short and spicy. Ask singers to visualize a garden hose with water flowing out the end; quickly slice through the stream of water with an index finger. This demonstrates how fast the consonants must be produced. Caution: consonants may become "too hot" and overemphasized. Another excellent technique to improve consonant rhythm is described in step 5 (tapping the sternum). Singers are to quickly place each consonant sound before the beat.

STEP 7. Fold vowels and consonants together to form syllables.
To quote Robert Shaw, "No two notes, syllables, or words should receive the same emphasis." This advice leads us to the next step in our entree—to determine the proper emphasis for each syllable within each word. Typically, second syllables receive less emphasis than first syllables. Singers who consistently emphasize the important syllables and "release" the unaccented syllables increase their connection to the poetry. Proper syllabic stress is the first step in the creation of an expressive phrase.

STEP 8. Dealing with foreign ingredients in the mix.
Our biggest challenge is the pronunciation of foreign words that may be unfamiliar to us. If possible, find someone who speaks the language. Next, transcribe the text into phonetic symbols using the International Phonetic Alphabet (IPA). Singers can learn IPA symbols very quickly, especially if the symbols are used in daily warm-ups. When singing a foreign language, it is also important to find a good literal translation. Read the translation several times and let the text simmer for a while. It will guide you to new rehearsal techniques that in turn will help singers make a deeper connection to the poetry.

STEP 9. Top each phrase with a dynamic shape.
After examining individual consonant and vowel sounds, as well as syllabic stress, the next step is to develop a plan for the each phrase. Each phrase has a specific dynamic shape that is often determined by the shape of the melodic line. The phrase grows toward a musical

and/or textual destination and then fades away. Each phrase in every vocal part is constantly moving; phrases are never static.

STEP 10. Diction al dente.

The final step is to look for and hopefully discover the words that touch our hearts. Where are they located in the poem? Are they set to quiet music or a dramatic *fortissimo*? How does the composer present the textual entree in combination with the other musical ingredients? When the text is carefully selected, examined, and prepared, choral musicians successfully communicate poetic and musical intent to their audiences. ➤

Learning About Music While Learning the Music

Lynn A. Corbin

"Learning the music" in a choral setting brings to mind several possible outcomes: mastering the notes and rhythms, producing good tone quality and expressive singing, memorizing the piece(s), or even working on theory or sight-reading. If we turn the phrase around and say "music learning," the same outcomes may appear, but the assessment and expectations might be somewhat different. What is it exactly that we "teach" in school choral ensembles? Or even better, what do the singers "learn"?

INGREDIENTS:
Process for teaching for music learning:

- Analyze repertoire for musical concepts and skills available for teaching.
- Describe the piece in detail: melody, harmony, rhythm, parts, text, form, texture, accompaniment.
- Select musical concepts and skills to teach.
- Develop objectives (first, middle, late rehearsals).
- Determine the sequence, focus, method, and manner of assessment.

SERVES:
Choral ensembles with expectations of an educational component.

In some detail, describe each musical element in a selected piece. The targeted element and the piece should be appropriate to the level of the ensemble. Develop specific statements of what students will be expected to know or be able to do based on the musical content found in selections from the repertoire. Some examples of objectives:

1. Students will perform Latin vowels correctly (pure, no diphthong, round and vibrant) and describe the vowels produced by the other sections, making appropriate suggestions for adjustment.
2. Students will utilize deep and controlled breathing throughout the piece, resulting in accurate intonation.
3. Students will listen and describe the dynamics as performed by other sections and evaluate the performance based on established performance practice. They will also describe the overall effect of these dynamic schemes on the piece.
4. Students will describe how they determine whether a chord is major or minor.

Organize rehearsal activities to address these objectives—early rehearsals have easier goals that build to accomplishing the objectives by the end of the rehearsal period. Each rehearsal should address at least one objective for that particular piece.

This recipe is especially effective for "authentic" assessment, a form of assessment that is embedded in the instructional experience. Quality assessment does not steal time from instruction, but rather, improves it. Students gain insight into what they are learning and how well they are doing. The following activities are suggested as embedded assessments that address the learning objectives presented earlier.

- **Vowels.** As students listen to each other and make suggestions as well as implement those given to them, the production of pure Latin vowels will be demonstrated.
- **Breathing**. As the intonation is maintained and phrases are performed correctly, deep and controlled breathing will be demonstrated.
- **Dynamics**. This is a two-step procedure. In the middle rehearsals, sections will experiment with various dynamic schemes, eventually arriving at one that they like. They will perform these and evaluate the effect. During subsequent later rehearsals, students will be made aware of Renaissance performance practice of dynamics. Each section will follow their volume levels using their arms—rising volume, rising arm; decreasing volume, lowering arm. You will be able to see during this activity whether the students know their line is rising or falling. They will also be able to see what the other sections are doing and how it all works together.
- **Major/minor**. Analyzing the quality of the chords at cadence points or other designated spots could be assigned as homework and collected. You could have students exchange scores and check each other's work. Section leaders could look to see if the homework was completed or if the scores had been marked during rehearsal as assigned. On demand, individual students on different days could identify verbally a major and/or a minor vertical harmony. The aforementioned physical gesture would work here also (hand up for major, arm straight out for minor).

These assessment activities are actually rehearsal activities during which the director makes note of the students' performance(s) and eventually assigns a grade. The objectives increase in level of expectation from early to late rehearsals, and the level of achievement increases with each rehearsal.

The concept of music learning embraces the notion that we are teaching more than "songs" in choir. Overlaying learning that goes beyond the mechanics enriches the experience and promotes the musicianship we claim is important. Singers learn what we offer in meaningful instructional ways, and they make the connections among the various aspects as we provide the means for them to do so. Assuming that performance alone fosters deep understanding is naïve. Performance enhanced with focused learning produces the understanding and musicianship we so strongly treasure and cherish.

Vowel Modification for a Resonant and Healthy Tone

R. Paul Crabb

Vocalists develop a rich, energized tone through proper vowel formation and resonance. This process becomes more complicated because the physical and acoustical demands change as the voice moves through low, middle, and high ranges. Are the sopranos supposed to sing a pure "ee" vowel [i] on g¹? Do the tenors sing a pure "ah" vowel [a] on top-line F-sharp? How can the conductor improve the sound *and* make it easier for the chorister to sing? Well-trained, experienced singers will naturally modify vowels in specific parts of their ranges, but less experienced singers may need advice on how to comfortably achieve focus and resonance through the lift areas of the voice. Vowel modification, especially in the passaggio and above the passaggio, solves many technical problems and intonation issues singers (and conductors) often encounter.

INGREDIENTS:

A conductor who knows the lift areas of each voice type and possesses sensitive, educated ears
Receptive choristers willing to try the ideas and suggestions of the conductor
Carefully designed warm-ups utilizing specific vowels and pitches found in the choir's repertoire, followed by direct application in the repertoire during rehearsal

SERVES:

This recipe can serve any number of singers of any age.

One role of the conductor is to facilitate and promote a resonant and healthy choral tone while simultaneously assisting singers to produce a relaxed, focused sound that encourages accurate intonation. How do conductors achieve this? Educated ears can hear correct vocal production when singers apply vowel modification, but more importantly, science supports these aural perceptions. As the respected vocal pedagogue Barbara Doscher said, "Vowel modification is the practical application of an acoustical law." (In *The Functional Unity of the Singing Voice.*, 2nd ed. Metuchen: Scarecrow Press, 1994. p. 165.)

The following chart provides suggestions for vowel modification of men's and women's voices. The conductor's knowledge of the voice and keen listening will determine the amount of modification that will vary in different areas of the voice.

Vowels are divided into two main categories: **lateral vowels** (sometimes called "front" or "closed" vowels) and **rounded vowels** (also called "back" vowels or "open" vowels). These definitions characterize the perceived location of the vowel formation in the mouth. Singers tend to feel the lateral vowel resonance/vibrations towards the front of the mouth and face, while rounded vowels may include additional vibratory sensations in the middle and back part of the mouth and head. Many vocal pedagogues advocate different modifications based on the gender of the singer.

Women

Female singers should add some of the vowel on the opposite side of the chart as they approach the passaggio. The percentage of the balancing vowel depends on the sensitive, informed ear of the listener. In the passaggio and above the passaggio, female singers use variations of the "ah" [ɔ] or "uh" [ʌ] vowel.

LATERAL VOWELS (front, closed)	ROUNDED VOWELS (back, open)
[i] (ee)	[u] (too)
[ɪ] (hit)	[ʊ] (full)
[e] (chaos)	[o] (toe)
[ɛ] (bet)	[ɔ] (awe)

Men

As the male singer approaches the passaggio, he should add some of the suggested vowel provided in the right hand column. Above the passaggio, closed vowel variants may work better for the lateral vowels; rounded vowels should be variants of [ʊ].

LATERAL VOWELS (front, closed)	
[i] (ee)	retain [i], may add [y] (German "ü")
[ɪ] (hit)	add [i]
[e] (chaos)	retain [œ], may add [ö] (German)
[ɛ] (bet)	add [e]
ROUNDED VOWELS (back, open)	
[u] (too)	pure for light sound, add [ʊ] for more sound
[ʊ] (full)	retain
[o] (toe)	add [ʊ]
[ɔ] (awe)	add [ʊ]
[ɑ] (father)	add [ʊ]

1. Doscher, Barbara M. *The Functional Unity of the Singing Voice.*, 2nd ed. Metuchen: Scarecrow Press, 1994, p. 165. ➤●

Enhancement of Choir Sound through Ensemble Spacing

James F. Daugherty

Space is a quality vital to the fullest experience of every art, says philosopher John Dewey (1859-1952). "Lack of room," he asserts, "is denial of life, and openness of space is affirmation of its potentiality." (In *Art as Experience*. New York: G. P. Putnam, 1934. p. 209.) Such appears to be the case with choir sound. While all sorts of variables contribute to the sound of particular choirs, empirical research finds that crowding singers together invariably has a negative impact upon their singing.

INGREDIENTS:
Basic principles of choir acoustics; self-to-other ratio; lateral and circumambient spacing

SERVES:
All choirs. Especially tasty to sopranos.

To lend your choir's sound a desirable nuance or, in some cases, a rather dramatic difference, try the following.

1. Position singers with sufficient space between them laterally, at least 18-24 inches or more.
2. When possible, grant singers circumambient space, another 18-24 inches behind and in front, in addition to lateral room.
3. To make the most of lateral and circumambient space, use a windowed arrangement so that no singer is standing directly in front of or behind another singer.
4. If there is room for only one voice section to spread out, attend first to the sopranos.
5. Because all choirs, singing venues, and literature sung are not alike, experiment to determine optimal spacing conditions for particular ensembles. Remember, using risers in performance does not mean that every singer has to be on them, or that each riser row must be occupied. If needed, allow some singers to spread out to the stage floor or proscenium steps, or even elsewhere in the auditorium, as conditions and sightlines to the conductor permit.
6. Consider that spacing requirements will vary according to the room acoustics of various venues. What works in the rehearsal room may not necessarily be ideal for the auditorium.

Understanding how distance between and among singers affects their combined sound is a key to experimenting with ensemble spacing. A major attraction of choir sound is the so-called "chorusing effect." Voices, in cooperation with prevailing venue acoustics, interact with such complexity that human ears dissociate the resulting conglomerate sound from its individual sources. This effect is both the appeal and the challenge of choral singing.

In chorusing, singers phonate and hear differently than they do as soloists. They attend simultaneously to two sounds: self-sound, or the airborne feedback of their own voices, and reference-sound, or the "chorused" sound of the rest of the ensemble. Choir singers have rather defined preferences with respect to this self-to-other ratio (SOR). Often, preference varies according to the frequencies sung (sopranos, for example, tend to have higher SOR preferences than basses), and where one stands in the choir (those standing at the ends of a choir have higher SOR preferences than those standing in the center portion of the choir). When reference sound overpowers self-sound, as happens when singers are crowded onto risers, problems ensue, including compensatory over-singing and poor intonation. Venue acoustics may exacerbate such problems. In overly absorbent rooms, for example, choir singers tend to raise their larynxes unless there is sufficient space between and among singers.

Controlled research studies indicate that choristers and auditors alike significantly prefer a choral sound achieved by putting more space between and among singers. This spacing preference appears to occur no matter which choir formation strategy is employed. Singers report more ease and efficiency in vocal production, although some less secure singers may be intimidated initially by circumambient spacing. Audiences report that the choir sound is more blended, balanced, and appealing.

Read More About It

Coleman, R. F. (1994). "Dynamic intensity variations of individual choral singers." *Journal of Voice, 8* (3), 196-201.

Daugherty, J.F. (1999). "Spacing, formation and choral sound: Preferences and perceptions of auditors and choristers." *Journal of Research in Music Education, 47* (3), 244-238.

Daugherty, J.F. (2001). "Rethinking how voices work in choral ensemble." *Choral Journal, 42* (5), 69-75.

Daugherty, J.F. (2003). "Choir spacing and formation: Choral sound preferences in random, synergistic, and gender-specific chamber choir placements." *International Journal of Research in Choral Singing, 1* (1), 48-59.

Hunter, E.J. (2004). "Overlap of hearing and voicing ranges, and a comparison of the VRP and the perceived VRP in singing." Paper presented at the Second International Physiology and Acoustics of Singing Conference, Denver, Colorado.

Rossing, T.D., Sundberg, J. & Ternström, S. (1986). "Acoustic comparison of voice use in solo and choir singing." *Journal of the Acoustical Society of America, 79* (6), 1975-1981.

Rossing, T.D., Sundberg, J. & Ternström, S. (1987). "Acoustic comparison of soprano solo and choir singing." *Journal of the Acoustical Society of America, 82* (3), 830-836.

Ternström, S. (1999). "Preferred self-to-other ratios in choir singing." *Journal of the Acoustical Society of America, 105* (6): 3563-3574.

Ternström, S. (2003). "Choir acoustics: An overview of research published to date." *International Journal of Research in Choral Singing, 1* (1), 3-12.

Ternström, S. & Karna, D. R. (2002). "Choir singing." In R. Parcutt & G.E. McPherson (eds). *The science and psychology of music performance: Creative strategies for teaching and learning.* New York: Oxford University Press.

Tonkinson, S. (1994). "The Lombard effect in choral singing." *Journal of Voice, 8* (1), 24-29. ➥

A Recipe for Sight-Singing Success

Steven M. Demorest

Music reading instruction is often portrayed as a chore that must be endured to get to the main course of rehearsing the literature. Many teachers feel it can also require a lot of special materials to begin working on sight-singing with their students. With a little imagination, it can be a fun appetizer or even a dessert, enjoyed by the entire ensemble. All it takes is a deck of cards.

INGREDIENTS:
A normal size or large deck of cards. Large cards can be found in many novelty shops. For all games, remove the face cards and the 9 and 10 cards, leaving Ace through 8 to represent the scale step numbers in a key or solfège syllables (1 = *Do*).

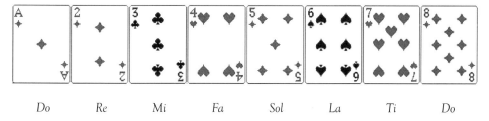

Do	*Re*	*Mi*	*Fa*	*Sol*	*La*	*Ti*	*Do*

The deck can then be "stacked" in different ways depending on the skill level of your ensemble. The most difficult level would be a full deck of every card, Ace through 8. This yields extremely challenging sequences involving lots of 7, 2, and 6 cards in patterns not often found in music and often starting on pitches other than the tonic. For very advanced groups, 9 and 10 can be added back in to extend the challenge beyond the octave. See specific cards to include for various levels in the recipes below.

SERVES:
Any choral ensemble with a beginning knowledge of numbers or solfège. Can also be prepared for two-person teams.

Nutritional Information
The game is a fun way to develop music-reading skills. It introduces a random element into reading scale patterns while adding the challenge of competition. You can "stack the deck" to feature certain intervals that students need to work on. If you wanted to focus on fourths you could add more 4 cards to the easy deck and remove other cards to increase the likelihood of getting fourths. You can also set up prearranged sequences or play games like "Name that Tune," where the cards are dealt one at a time until somebody can name the tune. It can be a

great teaching tool for students who are reading music on numbers. For those using solfège, it is a nice way to begin to connect the syllables to scale step numbers for harmony.

Easy Recipe
Cards to include: four Aces, one 2, two 3s, two 4s, three 5s. Take two Aces (tonic) and put them at the beginning and end of the sequence with six spaces in between, then deal out the other six cards at random. This way students can begin and end on the tonic.

Medium Recipe
Cards to include: four Aces, three 2s, three 3s, three 4s, four 5s, one 6, one 7, two 8s. This time put an Ace or 5 card at either end to help maintain key and vary the number of cards in between. This is a good level to begin "stacking the deck" for certain intervals (see below).

Hard Recipe
Cards to include: All cards Aces through 8s (also 9s and 10s, if desired). Again, the teacher can control key setting or even increase the challenge by having a certain preset pitch begin or end the sequence. At this level, try starting with eight cards dealt and then adding on to the sequence until somebody misses. At the top level, rhythms could be added to increase the difficulty. Write a rhythm pattern on the board and have students read it, then deal out a pitch sequence underneath each rhythmic value and read it again.

Serving a Large Group
The cards can be placed in the chalkboard tray or on music stands at the front of the room. Divide the choir into two or more teams (e.g., by section). The teacher or team leader shuffles the deck and then deals out eight cards in sequence. Each team has to read the sequence dealt to them correctly in order to get a point. Teams can either read the sequence as a group, or go down the line in *Family Feud* style, until somebody reads the sequence correctly.

To make starting and ending more consistent and to help with key setting, you can place an Ace (tonic) permanently at the beginning or end of the sequence then "deal" the other seven cards in sequence.

Serving for Two
A teacher can have a number of prepared decks available and do the card game in small groups or pairs, with students getting points for the number of correct sequences. It can even be a fun form of informal assessment with decks marked level 1–5, depending on the cards left in.

Read More About It
Demorest, S. M. (2001). *Building Choral Excellence: Teaching Sight-Singing in the Choral Rehearsal.* New York: Oxford University Press. ➡

How to Get Your Ensemble to Make M.U.S.I.C.

Rollo A. Dilworth

In today's choral community of conductors, composers, performers, and even consumers of the choral genre, much attention has been placed on the concepts of artistry and expression. What separates an outstanding choral performance from one that is just average? Aside from concepts such as "great diction," "perfect intonation," and "awesome balance and blend," I offer to you the following recipe for success.

INGREDIENTS:
The vocal or choral student must bring to the practice/rehearsal experience any score that needs to be prepared for performance.

SERVES:
All vocal/choral students.

M stands for **Mastery** of all pitches, rhythms, articulations, dynamics, pronunciations, etc. This is the first and perhaps the most basic step in the process. This step involves the mastery of every single note and mark that is on the printed page. Tedious as this may sound, it is extremely important to know what the composer is asking the performer to do. Keep in mind, however, that merely singing all of the right pitches at the right time does not automatically result in an artistically appealing performance.

U stands for the **Understanding** of text, context, and culture of the piece to be performed. It is extremely important that the conductor and singers understand the meaning of the text. We can often take the text for granted if it is written in English. Choose random moments in practice to ask singers to translate or paraphrase a portion of the text. This process ensures that the singer really has a grasp of not just the text itself, but the meaning or the intention behind the text. There may be multiple interpretations of the text, especially if the language is of a poetic or metaphoric nature. However, it is healthy to get some dialogue going amongst the choristers about the words they will eventually sing for an audience of listeners.

In terms of context, it is helpful for your singers to know, if possible, the context in which the piece was written. For example, was the piece composed during wartime, during the period of slavery, in preparation for a religious service, or for some other type of ceremony? Are there specific references to persons, places, or events in the piece? Third, we must take a careful look at the cultural context of the work. Language or dialect issues should be approached with sensitivity and sincerity. If at all possible, identify resources (recordings, IPA, native speakers) that will enable your singers to sound as authentic as possible. Also, try to understand how the piece functions within the culture that it represents.

S stands for **Soul**. Simply put, it is critical that your singers perform with some degree of energy and passion. I am convinced that every style of music—from Bach to rock—should be performed with some degree of soul. Do not settle for a performance that is technically perfect on one hand and lacking in drive and a sense of conviction on the other. I often equate choral performance to that of musical theater or opera performance. When singing a piece of choral music, the choristers (for the duration of the work) are essentially taking on the role or the mood of the person delivering the text. This concept of soul is sometimes difficult to describe, but one thing is for sure: most people know when your ensemble sings with it versus when they do not.

I stands for the **Internalization of Rhythm**. I have a sign on my bulletin board outside my office that says "External Rhythmic Precision Requires Internal Subdivision." Too often I have found myself as a conductor beating time and tapping the pulse for my singers. I would not have to do this very often if the singers would simply take responsibility for the underlying rhythmic pulsation of the piece. I think that it is quite easy for our ensembles to become dependent upon us as conductors to "keep the beat" for them. The ensemble will never learn to sing phrases expressively or sing attacks and releases with precision if they do not learn to feel the rhythmic subdivision for themselves. As a person who is sold on the Dalcroze Eurhythmics approach, I often make my singers move to the beat in rehearsal so that they can externalize the pulsation that is hopefully operating somewhere within their bodies.

Finally, **C** stands for **Communication**. Through the use of good diction (crisp consonants and tall vowels, for sure), appropriate facial gestures, and maybe even some other types of movement (emoting, sign language, body percussion, etc.), your singers have the awesome task of effectively communicating the style and character of the musical score. Sometimes these moods can shift from section to section or from phrase to phrase within a given work. This is why it is important to analyze the score in order to generate a thorough understanding of the text. In addition, your singers must effectively communicate the intentions of the composer through their performance. If the composer is deceased, conduct some research on performance practice for the period in question. If the composer is living, try to make contact with the person. ➤●

Soup & Salad: Improving Sight-Singing in Two Directions

Dwayne Dunn

While many school choir directors set aside a portion of their rehearsal time to work on sight-singing, much of this time is often spent reading melody lines in unison as a choir. While this is an appropriate diet for beginning sight-singers and young choirs, ultimately we want our singers to improve their sight-singing diet in two directions. First, we want them to become independent sight-singers who can read melody lines performing alone (soup). Secondly, we want our singers to be able to read in multiple parts simultaneously (salad), the way they encounter music that they are preparing to perform. Transitioning into these two important skill sets requires careful structure and planning, but pays off in improved ensemble accuracy, efficiency, and confidence.

INGREDIENTS:
Unison melody sight-singing exercises
Multipart chord progressions
Multipart sight-singing exercises
Black Sharpie marker
Poster board "Hall of Fame"

SERVES:
Intermediate to advanced sight-singers.

Basic Soup Recipe
Singers are often fearful of being asked to sing alone in front of the rest of the choir; being asked to *sight*-sing alone is an even more frightening prospect. As beginning sight-singers develop greater confidence and accuracy, look for ways to encourage choir members to sight-sing in smaller groups and eventually alone. A good beginning point may be to ask only one section of the choir at a time to sight-sing, perhaps changing sections with each new phrase or measure. Choristers can also be grouped by row, birthday month, shoe color, or any other method that pulls a small group of singers out of the large ensemble. If students are especially nervous about sight-singing in small groups, the director might begin with just the rhythm, having students clap or count-sing rhythm patterns in small groups, gradually moving toward adding pitch reading with stepwise scales.

Ask singers to read exercises that are at the appropriate difficulty level and length. A good starting place in a large group setting is to use exercises that contain mostly stepwise motion and leaps within the tonic chord and with a length of about eight measures of common time. As students gain confidence and mastery, increase difficulty levels incrementally for both pitch intervals and rhythmic patterns. As the choir becomes more comfortable with sight-singing in smaller and smaller groups, begin to ask for pairs of volunteers to try an exercise as a duet, and then ask for volunteer soloists. Enthusiastic applause should be a requirement from the entire group for any sight-singing duo or soloist. Because group support is such a crucial element in this process, have your choir practice applauding until you are pleased with the level of enthusiasm, then encourage that same level after every sight-singing attempt, regardless of how the performance turns out.

Devising games to encourage sight-singing alone is another great way to add an element of fun and focus to sight-singing, perhaps patterning rules after football, baseball, or other sports. Team games, where students can earn points for their team by sight-singing alone, are an excellent way to encourage camaraderie while sight-singing. Consider having exercises available at two or more difficulty levels, where students can attempt to earn more points for their team by choosing an exercise with a higher level of difficulty.

∾ *Extra Spicy Soup*
A sight-singing game that my choirs enjoy is one I "borrowed" from Brad White many years ago called "Paranoia." It is not intended for beginning sight-singers or as a first step toward sight-singing alone, but rather for students who have started to become comfortable with this skill. One of the selling points for this game is to help the choir realize that each person who plays is learning how to become a more independent sight-singer, and therefore is improving their contribution to the choir.

Early in the year, find one or two artistic students and commission a poster board called "The Hot Dog Hall of Fame," illustrated with hot dogs, musical symbols, red carpet icons, or with other creative designs. Leave a fairly large area blank. Students who sight-sing one exercise alone with accurate pitch, rhythm, and tonal syllables (*Do-Re-Mi* or numbers) will sign their name to the Hall of Fame in the blank area. Mount the Hall of Fame poster where everyone can see it and reach it.

Choose an exercise that singers are able to read fairly well as a class; I am fond of the tunes in Oxford's *The Folk Song Sight Singing Series*, but any appropriate exercises of about eight measures will work. Begin by determining the location of the tonic, verifying the meter, looking for unusual leaps or rhythms, and establishing the tonic key in our voices (*Do-Mi-Sol-Mi-Do* for major). Have the group sing through the exercise together twice, taking a few seconds between readings to point out any places that caused problems and suggest solutions. The readings do not have to be perfect, but if the group cannot keep a steady beat and get to the end of the exercise without major problems, the exercise is too difficult for this game.

On the first day, everyone is eligible to play. Each successive time you play, those who already played cannot be called on again until everyone else has taken a turn, which completes one round. To keep the selection process somewhat random, the leader calls an eligible chorister's name and begins counting to 5, during which the person whose name was called will call on another member, who will call on another, and so on, without repeating any of the names already called and without calling someone who has completed this round. The last name called before the leader gets to "5" then auditions for the Hot Dog Hall of Fame. The leader can vary the tempo and rhythm of the counting each time so that the singers will not be able to predict when "5" will be called. If an ineligible person for that round is called, that person automatically gets the opportunity to audition. Each day, fewer and fewer choir members are eligible, until eventually, the last person called has no other name to call. Some singers will get creative at this point and call the conductor's name. When my singers do that, I usually play the game and sight-sing the exercise to show them that this is an important skill for me as well.

For the audition, hold up the Sharpie pen (we call him "Mr. Pen"), and help the student find their starting pitch (you can sing this with them). Allow them to set their own tempo and begin the exercise, holding the pen straight up. As long as they maintain the correct pitch, rhythm, and syllable names, allow them to keep going and continue to hold the pen up. If they falter, put the pen down or into your breast pocket, and help them continue until they finish the exercise. Some students will get right back on track and finish without any help, while others may need you to sing every note with them. Regardless, *everyone will finish the exercise*, after which the class will erupt into enthusiastic applause. If the pen is still standing at the end, the person was successful and may take the pen and sign the Hall of Fame. This is such a momentous event that we keep clapping for them until they finish signing. Typically, only one or two singers get to audition each time we play.

While a person is auditioning for the Hall of Fame, all other choir members should practice their Curwen hand signs, as this keeps their focus on the music rather than the person singing. If I catch someone who is not practicing their hand signs, they have to stand and sing next. Be firm about what constitutes a successful performance. If the exercise ends with a whole note, the singer must hold the note four full beats, no more and no less. Remind the other students not to applaud prematurely and disrupt their concentration. I have had rounds where only one or two singers in the entire choir made it onto the Hall of Fame, because it is difficult to sight-sing alone, even for the best readers. Sometimes it is good for the weaker readers in the choir to see that even the best students find it challenging to sight-sing alone.

Stocking the Salad Bar
For students who possess basic unison sight-singing ability, the transition to multipart reading can be challenging. Begin by making sure students are singing a part that is comfortable for their vocal range, and start with two- and three-part harmonic progressions with little or no rhythmic difficulty (all quarter notes except for longer notes at the end of a phrase). Keep the tempo fairly slow, about one quarter note per second. It may seem like a big step back from what the singers are capable of sight-singing as a unison choir, but the challenges of tuning chords and mastering rhythmic precision while singing multiple parts will take much of their mental focus. If the music is too difficult at this point, singers will be less willing to apply their sight-singing skills to multipart music.

Encourage each section to first figure out the tonal syllables for their part, and then look for places they will either match another part, or as the music advances in difficulty, where they will clash with another part. Look for sections within your concert repertoire that can be read directly or modified by simplifying the rhythm to be sung on tonal syllables. In a four-part choir, pair different sets of voices together to simplify the act of sight-singing if four parts are too many at first. Be on the hunt at all times for pieces of music that offer opportunities for the choir to apply their reading skills directly to their concert repertoire. As they become more comfortable and skilled in sight-singing, they will begin to ask you to let them learn new literature using their tonal syllables because they know it improves their pitch and rhythm accuracy. ➤●

Table of Acceptable Substitutes: Turning Score Terminology into Expressions

Morna Edmundson

Some of our favorite recipes, while still effective, tasty, and steeped in cherished tradition, could do with a makeover. Try some of the following on your choir. The less the substitute has to do with music, the more effective it can be. Your singers will smile, they may think you are crazy, but they will also sing differently—with more of a spring in their vocal step—and your rehearsal will be that much lighter, fluffier, and have longer-lasting results.

INGREDIENTS:
See recipe below.

SERVES:
For all choirs; especially beginning musicians yet to learn terminology.

Most conductors have discovered their own fabulous substitutes—the possibilities are endless. Try these out, share them with others, and invent your own. You'll be glad you did.

Traditional Ingredient:	Acceptable Substitutes:
poco a poco accelerando	like a shopping cart in a sloped parking lot
pesante	like a medicine ball landing on a water bed
mezzo piano	with a little fat on its bones
mezzo forte	joyous and extroverted
	you're the narrator; tell the story with intention and great diction
	relaxed and full; physically very free
forte	ecstatic
	like a diva!
ritardando	let the energy evaporate into thin air
leggiero	like one of those water spiders that manages to walk nimbly along on top of the water without falling in
più mosso	eagerly; you can't wait to get there
legatissimo	sing like Gaston does in the Disney movie *Beauty and the Beast*
pianissimo	sing like you do when you're washing the dishes and someone comes into the room and says, "Oh, I like that song" and you realize for the first time that you were singing out loud but very much for yourself ➞

Eight Essential Ingredients for Preparing Choirs for Performance

Kevin Fenton

Gesture, motivation, score study, stylistic understanding, and rehearsal methods are all essential aspects of the art of choral conducting. Conductors who focus on technique without motivation lead musical performances that lack expression. Conductors who focus on gesture without thorough knowledge of the score or stylistic understanding lead musical performances that lack meaning. The use of the following eight techniques will ensure that singers will perform expressively and meaningfully.

INGREDIENTS:
No "kitchen" should be without these essential techniques.

SERVES:
All ages and types of choirs.

TECHNIQUE 1. Develop true unity through the use of nonsense syllables.
In early rehearsals of a piece, establish the tone quality that represents the mood or character of the piece by utilizing a nonsense syllable depicting the conductor's aural image. For example, for a renaissance *Ave Maria*, the aural image of tone might be "sweet" and "uniform." Help singers create the desired tone by having the choir sight-read the piece using "doo" or "noo" or "neh" or "deh." By eliminating the complexities of text, singers can focus on producing a unified sound with the appropriate tone—the conductor's aural image.

TECHNIQUE 2. Develop unified phrase movement through the use of gesture.
Determine and utilize melded gestures (vague or soft ictus points) to display the movement and character of sustained pitches. Use active gestures to display phrase lifts or rhythmic motion of a musical line. Dynamics and strong and weak syllables can be displayed by adjusting the height of the ictus (lower icti for strong beats and higher icti for weak beats). Rely on gesture rather than verbal instructions to allow singers to develop their own musical intuition in the music-making process and to allow conductors and singers flexibility to make adjustments in performance in response to acoustics.

TECHNIQUE 3. Use gesture to communicate the concept of transparency.
When conducting polyphony, focus not on the entire choir but on the different voice parts within the choir. Through gesture, encourage the vocal part that is executing thematic mate-

rial to become dominant or indicate to sections without thematic material the need to diminish. Approaching and responding to individual voice parts within the choir will promote the transparency that is essential for creating clarity in polyphonic music.

TECHNIQUE 4. Use echo chanting and rhythmic chanting to demonstrate pure and open vowels, and to display a lifted approach to vowel production.
The value of echo chanting goes beyond the rudimentary teaching of diction and helps the singer on many levels. Echo chanting helps singers understand the difference between the speaking voice and the singing voice by modeling text using a lifted tone and displaying a singer's posture. Displaying phrase movement and stressed and unstressed syllables during echo chanting is often more efficient than verbal explanations.

TECHNIQUE 5. Use the layering technique to keep rehearsals efficient and engaging.
When teaching singers difficult sections of music, conductors have often relied on sectional rehearsals that leave many students uninvolved. The layering technique allows conductors to teach rhythm and pitches while keeping members of all voice parts engaged.

Here's how it works. Begin with one voice part (altos for this example) singing a one- to four-bar phrase with piano. After the read through, isolate specific intervals or rhythms performed incorrectly and use modeling, echo chanting, or intervallic cues to correct the mistakes. Once the altos master pitches and rhythms, move to the second voice part (soprano section for this example), singing the same section with the piano, followed by isolation work. Then *layer* the two parts by asking the altos and sopranos to sing together. Use the same process with tenors and basses, then complete the sequence with all four voice parts singing together. You will be amazed by the accuracy. Instructions during this process should be brief and the focus should be only pitches and rhythms. A typical layering sequence takes no longer than 4 minutes to complete.

TECHNIQUE 6. Maintain "positive impatience" in rehearsal.
Display **positive impatience** by using concise and proactive directions such as, "Basses, bar 22 the rhythm is doo-doot-doot-doo," or "Altos: think of the G-sharp as a leading tone to the A-natural." Teach singers solutions without dwelling on problems by using activities that guide singers to the correct performance. To maintain positive impatience during the rehearsal, stop the choir only after determining exactly what method will be used to correct or improve the performance. This creates a rehearsal atmosphere that is positive, yet still addresses details of artistic singing.

TECHNIQUE 7. Use stories related to the composer or the inspiration of the composition to motivate singers.
The message of text, the intent of the composer, and the circumstances surrounding the creation of a composition can do a great deal to motivate and inspire singers. Such information can come in the form of short stories or one-sentence association cues, and they can provide refreshed energy in singers and their performance when utilized after the pitches and rhythms have been mastered.

TECHNIQUE 8. Use a speaking voice that depicts the expression of the music.
Create an atmosphere in rehearsals consistent with the character of the music being rehearsed by speaking about a *forte* section while speaking *forte* or by speaking softly with energy when rehearsing a *pianissimo* section. Use analogies to motivate singers to sing with appropriate character. The goal is to inspire singers to be expressive and to perform with purpose and passion. The speaking voice is an important tool. ➤

Stocking the Shelves for a Full Cupboard of Vowels

Janet Galván

Vowels are to the conductor as flour is to the baker. By working on vowels, the choral conductor can solve a multitude of problems. The choice of whether to use a dark vowel (whole wheat), a bright vowel (self-rising), or just a beautiful standard *bel canto* vowel (plain white flour) depends on the composition, culture, style, period, or dramatic effect. However, all singers need to be in agreement about the vowel. Matching vowels can go a long way toward creating what we like to think of as choral blend. Vowels are the backbone of tone. Therefore, much technique can be taught through good vowel work.

INGREDIENTS:
A good singing model
A good set of ears
A choir
High standards for sound
Consistency in warm-up and repertoire portions of the rehearsal
Knowledge of the formation of vowels, including diphthongs and triphthongs

SERVES:
The singing voice, the sound of the choir, and each section within the choir; the composition; the communication of the language; blend.

Each day the conductor spends time listening in warm-ups. Warm-ups are not done in a mindless fashion but as an instruction for further refinement of vocal technique and skills of musicianship. The teacher listens and gives feedback about vowel formation, vowel matching, and the sound, but also asks guided questions so that the students begin to listen critically across the chorus.

The conductor works from vowels that lead one vowel to the other with ease (high to low, front to back, etc.) to allow the students to feel the movement. Vowels that are produced with the tongue closer to the roof of the mouth are described as high vowels. Back and front describes where in the mouth the tongue approaches the roof of the mouth. Specific instructions should be given according to what is heard. If the sound of the chorus is too covered, the teacher might start with a high, forward vowel and move to the low, back vowel with a trace of the high forward vowel in the production. If the sound is thin and too bright, the conductor might work from a low, back vowel. The conductor should be sure that the singing begins on the breath. Just as you would not try to cook a cake with no heat, one would not want to form vowels with no breath.

The conductor should also observe how singers look as they are singing. If the jaw is jutted forward in a tense position, the conductor will know that the vowels are not being sung in a free, healthy manner.

A good vowel to work on head voice for younger singers is the "oo" vowel [u]. This is a high back vowel. The "oo" vowel is formed with the tongue approaching the roof of the mouth in the back of the mouth. Using the "oo" vowel on a siren for warm-up allows students to feel the sensation of the space in the upper mouth (slightly raised soft palate), which helps them feel the sensation of head voice. One can work from the feel of the "oo" to other vowels.

In teaching vowels, use visual kinesthetic and aural ideas. In working with the "oo," one can have students work in pairs. If their lips are rounded, the partner gives a thumbs-up sign. If the lips are not rounded and are spread sideways, the students form a circle around their mouths to show their partner that they need more roundness. One can also have the students draw a circle in front of their mouths as they sing. The teacher can demonstrate the unrounded and the rounded sound so that students can hear the difference.

Singers are able to understand single vowel sounds, diphthongs, and triphthongs at an early age. During the repertoire portion of the rehearsal, the conductor needs to continue to listen to the vowels. Singing on vowels only is a good technique to isolate and refine the vowel sounds. Chanting the correct speech in a higher pitch is a good way to work vowel sounds. Echo work, with the teacher saying vowel sounds correctly and incorrectly, helps students feel the sensation of the correct production and how it differs from incorrect production. Having one section sing as another section listens and offers constructive comments is a good way to make everyone more aware of the effect of vowel production and vowel matching.

Working on vowels within the context of repertoire is helpful because it is in a meaningful context. It is important that the conductor listen carefully as students sing. If the tone is less than desirable, vowels are often at least part of the problem. If everyone is singing beautiful vowels, the chorus will have a more beautiful sound. If everyone understands how to sing beautifully rounded, long, tall *bel canto* vowels, they can then be altered as needed—brighter for some repertoire, darker for others. ➥

Spice Up Your Warm-Ups

Mary Goetze

The warm-up structure is rather like the pyramid of foods. Where you have fruits and veggies, meats, eggs, dairy, carbs, and fats in daily diet, your warm-up regimen should include exercises for posture, breathing, resonance, and articulation. However, I often run out of engaging ideas for these major exercise groups. That is when I try spicing up the warm-up by adding thoughtful questions.

INGREDIENTS:
Questions that prompt musical problem solving while enhancing musical understanding and skills

SERVES:
For making the warm-ups thoughtful and engaging for any age choir, but especially for musicians or children who can benefit from applying new vocabulary and musical concepts.

Ask a "What if . . . ?" question. For instance, sing this pattern:

Then ask, "What if the meter were 3/4 instead of 4/4?" Have the choir conduct in 3/4, and ask them to imagine how it would sound if the melody fit this new meter. Then invite individuals to sing it aloud or let everyone sing their idea all at once. You might hear:

or some other variation. Have the choir describe the differences in the responses, and repeat them. Some may be hesitant to sing alone, but keeping the focus of attention on the question and the musical response rather than on judging the voice or the person will build their trust in you and their confidence at the same time. Here are some other possible "what if . . .?" questions:

- What if this melody went up instead of down?
- What if it were in minor instead of major?
- What if these steps were 3rds?

- What if it were twice in augmentation? (or diminution)?
- What if the sopranos sang it starting on the third of the scale and the altos on the tonic?
- What if we sang it in a canon?

Another favorite question of mine assists the conductor and the choristers to become better acquainted. Sing a vocalise on "*si si si*," such as:

Repeat it on various pitches, then ask, "In what language does that word mean 'yes?'" Ask them to share how to say "yes" in other languages then sing them to the same pattern. Have them decide if the character might be different for the new language. For instance, should it be staccato or legato? Forte or piano? Or perhaps the melody might ascend instead of descend first. This is a nice way to find out what languages are spoken by choristers—and it might make an international student feel valued and welcomed. I am always amazed to learn that students today know Japanese (*hai*), Russian (*da*), German (*ja*), Portuguese (*sim*), or French (*oui*).

It takes but a few seconds for them to remake the vocalise to fit such changes, and while the voice is exercised, vocabulary is reviewed, prepared, or introduced, and minds are engaged in problem solving. ━●

Old-Fashioned Learning-Tree Stew: Good for Building Honor, Respect, and Self-Esteem

Stephanie Bartik Graber

With all the technological advances of the twenty-first century, sometimes it seems we are more detached from our students than ever before. In ancient times, the master sat in the shade of a tree and taught a student about truth and beauty. The exchange was special, important, unique, and personal—food for thought. In today's world, one might wonder just how well we truly connect with each other, one to one. Do our students know that each and every one of them is important to us and that, in a unique way, they are each the soul of the group? Each one adds their own special *spice* to the group and even to our lives. How can we help each of our students know that we "see" them and acknowledge them as unique and important?

INGREDIENTS:
Faces, all kinds and shapes
Teacher's eyes = caring
Student's eyes = focused
Individual "spices" that each student brings to the group
Concentrated effort of ingredient preparation that requires "looking" into each student's eyes with eyes that can "see"
Slow cooking that produces a sense of time and place and individual attention
Low heat, which enhances a sense of proactive recognition
Stir evenly in the form of a figure-8 to produce the realization of lifelong relationships
Top with an ample helping of altruism

SERVES:
One at a time.

How can we help our students build the self-esteem so necessary for success in all of life's endeavors? The truth is we are all getting less and less of the attention we need from each other these days. Meeting students where they are, with their esteem needs and at their current stage of intellectual development, validates for each student a teacher's sincere effort on their behalf.

That's when the eyes go to work. Whenever I really need to make my students "hear" or "connect" with me, I say, "Give me your eyes." The Roman orator and statesman Cicero said, "The face is a picture of the mind as the eyes are its interpreter." Later came the French saying, "The eyes are the mirror of the soul." As choir directors, we have always understood the important effect our choirs' facial expressions and eye contact have on an audience. But think about it . . . do you ever find yourself in a rehearsal "glazing over" and on automatic pilot? In today's fast-paced existence, do we take the time to look our students in their eyes with a depth and breadth of connection? Do we really see who they are and how special they are? Do our students really, truthfully "see" and hear us?

Our world is one of rapid change and what the post-modern philosophers call "hyper-reality." We need more than ever before to be making a positive personal connection with our students. We, as teachers, need to show them, guide them, and share with them those time-tested, universal, and golden secrets of the learning-tree method. Let them know through our eyes that we "see" their potential, and recognize and realize their uniqueness . . . that we celebrate their existence and involvement.

Remember . . . if you do not have their eyes . . . the give and take of effective communication is not fully engaged, honor and respect not realized. The "eyes" have it!

Bon appétit.

Leaven to Counteract Loafing: Developing a Self-Responsible and Collaborative Choir

Alan J. Gumm

Whenever many work together, as in a choir, individuals tend to feel less needed and therefore contribute less to the group experience or loaf around and leave the work to others. This social loafing was first detected in 1913 in French engineer Ringelmann's research of individual effort in a tug-of-war rope pull. It was first applied to choral music in Stocker's April 1981 *Choral Journal* article, and can be counteracted using any number of the "leaven" recipes I have compiled and developed over my career. As leaven allows a substance to rise, enliven, and increase in volume, these recipes will help give rise to individual responsibility, leadership, and interdependent teamwork in a choir.

INGREDIENTS:

Practice rooms for each section of the choir or a rehearsal room large enough for small group work, a piano, an ability to detect leadership abilities in students, and optional labeled slips of paper to assign leadership roles:

- Initiator—helps to get tasks started and moving along
- Information Giver—shares knowledge of music
- Gate Keeper—helps decide turn taking
- Time Keeper—helps the group keep track of time and get things done on time
- Involver/Opinion Seeker—keeps everybody alert and contributing
- Encourager—helps convince hesitant group members to contribute
- Praiser—acknowledges good ideas and efforts
- Clarifier—notices when ideas or directions are unclear and helps explain clearly
- Elaborator—clarifies or expands on others' ideas
- Peacemaker—helps resolve conflict so the group stays positive and productive

SERVES:

Choral directors ready to share leadership for deeper results.
All choir students, ready or not.

Full-Choir Recipe

To build a strong group dynamic, each member can be given a unique role to carry out in the full choir. This can be a unique **leadership** role (see list of ingredients) that can be recognized, pointed out, and encouraged in each choir member or handed out on slips of paper as an assignment. For instance, "I noticed how you tend to help by . . . so can you keep working at this skill to help everybody?" Or on the other hand, "I have a new skill for each of you to try that will help the entire choir . . ."

A unique musical role can be assigned by arranging the members of each section from dark to light **voice color** so everybody learns how each distinct color contributes to the overall choral tone. Choir members can be matched up by **voice strength** and **music reading** ability so a strong voice can help encourage a more reserved voice and a good reader can help a neighbor learn to read. When it comes closer to concert time, choir members can be asked to self-rate their level of **memorization** on a scale of 1 to 5, share ratings visually on raised hands, and rearrange themselves in an order that best influences the entire section.

Any change in the **seating/standing arrangement**, whether by following the suggestions above or simply by rotating rows periodically, keeps choir members alert by changing their proximity to the conductor and each others' influence. To further spread the conductor's influence around, get away from the podium and **circulate** at unexpected times to gain closer proximity to each individual, checking not so much that they are following the conductor's lead but that they are taking personal initiative in helping the choir.

Small Group Recipe
The group dynamic of a choir can benefit from various collaborative small group activities. The leadership roles practiced in full choir can be put into play for successful **sectional rehearsals**; instead of one section leader, each member carries out a different leadership role. Sectionals can be held in separate rooms with the conductor going from room to room to help maintain leadership roles, or sections can stand or sit in separate circles around the main rehearsal room, with each person sharing problems identified in the score and working collaboratively to prioritize errors and solve problems.

Peer performance can also enhance group dynamics, with an individual or small group demonstrating a section of the music or a vocal technique to be perfected by everybody. Choir members can be asked to pair up, critique a neighbor, and suggest improvements. Paired or small-group brainstorming can be used so all choir members get to share an idea with someone else—the topic can be anything from a definition of terminology to interpretation of the text—and then the group can share the best ideas with the entire choir. With each of these strategies, everybody contributes an idea and the best ideas come to the attention of all.

Once choir members realize their unique leadership role, voice color, voice strength, reading ability, and ability to memorize, they have what it takes to develop individual chamber ensembles from within the choir. Skills learned as a member of a trio or quartet go back into making the choir experience that much more self-responsible and collaborative, and well worth the effort and time. Come festival or concert time, extra performance ensembles already exist as part of a collaborative educational process. ➤●

Turning Thoughts into Words: Writing to and with Your Choir

Paul D. Head

It is not unusual that the soft-spoken freshman in the back row actually has a lot to say, but never feels comfortable expressing himself verbally in front of others. And conversely, the conductor may benefit by sharing her innermost thoughts, but stopping the rehearsal to do so is simply neither practical nor productive. Finding a way to facilitate written communication *to* and *within* your ensemble will help each musician consider and develop unique images and ideas as related to the musical score.

INGREDIENTS:
Required: A choir and a director that desires to foster meaningful musical experiences for the ensemble *and each individual* therein
Optional: Paper, pencils, markers, imaginative questions, a computer with Internet access, an Internet forum page, or even a simple e-mail list

SERVES:
All choir students, and ultimately the audience too.

One might say that this is a variation on a recipe that was so very successful for Robert Shaw as he wrote to his choruses on a regular basis about music, about life, about religion and philosophy, and even about last night's rehearsal.

While this recipe lists only one required ingredient, remember that limiting yourself to just this one ingredient may not create the dessert that you ultimately crave. If you are craving a choir that is fully engaged in the musical process, then you must find a way for each member of that choir to become an active ingredient in the final mixture. Some might say that too many cooks spoil the broth, but when it comes to the integration of many ideals, beliefs, and backgrounds, there is a compelling case to be made for drawing on the collective expertise of every human's unique perspective and experience. But how?

First, we must create opportunities for our singers to write. Consider the last five minutes at the end of each Wednesday's rehearsal—hand them a piece of paper and put them to task. Of course, thoughtful answers are typically inspired by thought-provoking questions. "Is there evidence in the music that Poulenc wrote this during the War?" "Is it by accident that Thompson doesn't let the basses sing the root of the chord?" "Do you share the same interpretation of that text as does Mr. Handel?" Most of us will need to experiment with a taste of this and a dash of that until we are able to create questions that appropriately rise when fully baked.

Secondly, we must find time to read what our sing
public forum for those who are able to provide un
you will have a student who is an expert on the poe
the summer acting in a Shakespeare company. An
nobody else, including yourself, could have ever the
e-mail and ask students to add to the discussion an
on a free message board provided by your institutio
MSN. Or if you publish a weekly newsletter to you
leted remarks excerpted from what your students h
you can make sure that you never leave a single ing

Allow this to bake over the course of a semester
ference in the involvement and buoyancy of your
our singers to rely on the conductor's impassioned
minds to soar as together we face the challenges of turning one-dimensional notation into an
expression of life, love, and humanity. ➥

Superior Stew: How to Achieve Top Ratings at Choral Festivals

Michael D. Huff

During the school year, especially in the spring, most school choirs participate in festivals or contests in which they are evaluated by a panel of adjudicators and given a score or rating based on their performance. A "superior" rating can do much to increase enthusiasm and exertion amongst the singers, enhance the reputation and influence of the conductor, and encourage parents and administrators to continue and even increase their support of the school's choral music program. My experience as Artistic Director of The Festival of Gold™ Series and as a frequent adjudicator at choral festivals throughout the country has convinced me that most adjudicators are looking for the same thing: **good literature artfully sung**. Here is the recipe:

INGREDIENTS:
1 fairly balanced chorus
3–5 well-crafted, attainable pieces of music
Equal portions:
- formalized, resonant vowels
- clear, energized consonants
- expressive, artful phrases
- personal commitment
- conductor's musical preparation

SERVES:
Choirs of all ages whose aim is to have excellence reflected in scores received at festivals or competitions in which numerical scores or ratings are given.

Whether you have an auditioned chorus of highly accomplished singers, or a "ya'll come" group of enthused vocalists, achieving a "superior" rating is entirely possible. The first step is for you, through consistent encouragement and instruction, to set the highest possible standard for vocal production, and never retreat from that standard.

Most students are capable of singing the same pitches (how many "true tenors" do you know?), so *you* can control sectional balance by assignment. With your choir in place, choose festival pieces that will play to your choir's strengths in terms of balance, technique, and musicianship. **Helpful Hint:** Make sure that the music you choose can stand the test of time. Avoid pieces that are trite.

Throughout the school year, whether preparing for the upcoming Christmas concert or (especially) working on your festival literature, have as your choir's mantra the following recipe ingredients:

- formalized, resonant vowels
- clear, energized consonants
- expressive, artful phrases

You will find that the physical demands associated with open-throated (i.e., *bel canto*) singing, along with energized diction, will yield associated benefits of improved intonation and a collectively well-focused vocal tone. Making these principles the foundation of your choir's sound will ultimately lead to less time spent solving vocal problems and more time exploring the expressive possibilities of the great music you have chosen to sing!

The entire process of achieving excellence in musical performance requires an undeviating personal commitment, exemplified by the conductor and shared by every singer. This commitment must embody a collective determination to master the technical demands associated with beautiful singing: muscular support of a well-managed stream of air; relaxed and efficient adduction of vocal folds; open, flexible resonators; and energized articulators (lips, teeth, tongue). It must also embody the choir's willingness to project themselves out to the audience by leaving no question in any listener's mind as to the content and meaning of the piece being sung.

All of these ingredients must be combined under the guidance of a conductor who has done his/her "homework" by identifying the musical and compositional elements that make the chosen music great. This means finding precisely the right tempo for the music, executing dynamics with precision, assuring that all the notes are balanced and in place, and considering and solving all interpretive questions, thus assuring that the music will be faithfully rendered and the singers' artistic horizons expanded. Do all of these things over the course of your school year, and your "superior" is in the bag! ◆

Preparing the Mind, Preparing the Ear: Developing Subvocalization Skill to Improve Intonation

Eric A. Johnson

While considering the many needs of your choral ensemble it is difficult to overstate the importance of hearing and singing with accurate intonation. The most beautifully shaped phrase, performed with great energy and commitment, can be quickly undermined by an out-of-tune interval or chord. Oh how we loathe those "low pressure" days when the energy of the choir is such that nothings rings true. But what are you to do? Where do you begin to unwrap the many layers of vocal production that play central roles in intonation?

INGREDIENTS:
Subvocalization skills of moving every muscle necessary to make a sound up to the point of phonation (inhalation, moving tongue, lifting soft palate, etc.) to improve the connection between the inner ear and the voice
Creatively engaged minds
Willingness to move away from the piano

SERVES:
Singers of all ages who are working on sight-reading skills or want to refine their intonation.
Directors who want to improve their own audiation skills.
Can be used in any musical style or context.

Of the myriad of factors that impact our singers' ability to sing in tune—posture, breath support, vowel placement/color/uniformity, rhythmic vitality, or muscle tension—an even more basic concept often overlooked and frequently subverted is how to prepare the singer's mind to hear and reproduce pitches *before* they are sung.

> ˜ *If we want our singers to sing in tune, they have to think in tune.* ˜

In every stage of vocal instruction it is important to develop strategies to engage the singer's mind in the process of generating and maintaining pitch. An active inner ear is an imperative element of accurate intonation, but it also needs to be connected to the vocal process, which can sometimes be a challenge to our students. Subvocalization helps develop and strengthen the connection between the inner ear and the voice and ultimately becomes an empowering tool for lifelong singing.

In early stages of connecting the inner ear to the vocal process, be patient with your students. Give them time to internalize and subvocalize. Subvocalizing allows students to evaluate their own pitch accuracy before they actually generate a sound, improves pitch memory, and develops the singer's ability to hear tonality over extended periods of time. Initially, some students may struggle with internalizing a single pitch. Hearing multiple notes (harmonic intervals, triads, etc.) is an advanced skill that takes time to develop, but one that will not develop on its own.

Teach students to imagine different internal sound sources, or carriers, when audiating a pitch. Singers tend to hear their own voice when they imagine sounds. If the initial pitch is out of their vocal range it is harder to generate a clear auditory image. However, that same pitch imagined as played on the piano may come very easy to the ear. This can be especially useful during the high-mutation stage of voice change, where most points of reference in the voice may be completely lost.

As much as possible, warm-ups and rehearsals should be conducted without the use of the piano. If you do use a piano during warm-ups, give only starting pitches for familiar patterns or play only the harmonic functions in the exercise, not the exact notes sung. Ideally, students should be able to find the starting pitch of a new vocalise by subvocalizing the last pitch sung and the target pitch (e.g., start a fourth higher). We need to teach students processes they can use to mentally shift among keys, rather than rely on the piano to modulate for them. If students aren't challenged to hear independently, they won't.

Subvocalization Applications in Warm-ups
- While singing a familiar tonal pattern, add random subvocalization. On a specific cue the singers stop making sound but continue to subvocalize the pattern. At the next cue the singers resume singing the pattern as if they had never stopped making sound.
- Subvocalize an entire vocal exercise, but randomly stop and have the choir sing the next pitch in the pattern.
- When singing familiar patterns modulate to unpredictable keys (e.g., C major, F-sharp major, A minor, etc.). This activity keeps the singers mentally engaged in generating new tonal centers that are far removed from the previous keys.
- Sing a major scale by section (soprano = *Do*, alto = *Re*, tenor = *Mi*, etc.). This is an advanced activity and really requires the singers to subvocalize all of the pitches so that *their* entrances are accurate.
- Repeat the preceding exercise but instruct the students to sustain their pitch until their next note to be sung in the scale.
- Sing patterns against sustained notes (e.g., bass and alto sustain *Sol* while soprano and tenor sing *Sol-Fa-Mi-Re-Do*). This enforces the importance of hearing the tonal center. Intervals are not disjunct events, but are heard and understood as part of an underlying harmonic context.

Advanced Subvocalization Activities
- Always give the students time to internalize the tonal center of a work (i.e., subvocalize *Do, Ti, Do, Sol, Do*). Simply hearing a key-defining pattern played on a piano does not ensure that the students have actually internalized the new tonal center.

- Once a tonality is established for a work, do not constantly give starting pitches to the ensemble. Encourage them to remember the tonal center in their heads. This takes time and concentration, but it can be done!
- Make certain that singers know the tonal center for each song or section of a song. If they aren't "hearing" a modulation—they have the wrong harmonic context— that means they are hearing that section in the wrong key.
- Teach singers to think and hear harmonically by accompanying exercises and compositions with chords. In time, the accompaniment can be taken away and the students will still be able to recall the sound of the underlying harmony. In this way, the students have the correct harmonic context for the given passage. It is very difficult for a young singer to sing *Sol-Re* if the tonal image they have is a tonic *Sol-Mi-Do*. If you teach them to hear the dominant function, however, *Sol-Re* will be consistently more accurate.

Read more about Johnson & Klonoski's research on this topic in the October 2003 *Choral Journal.*

Choir Curry: Seasoning for Success

Michael Jothen

Choirs, in different styles, shapes, and forms, exist for different purposes and reasons. The Bach Singers, Chancel Choir, Symphonic Chorus, The Renaissance Motet Choir, Sanctuary Choir, The Schola Cantorum, Children's Choir, The New Music Ensemble, Adult Choir, The Avant Garde Singers, The Motivational Singers, The Seniorizors, Youth Choir, Chorale, Glee Club, and A Cappella Choir are just some of the varied names used by choirs. Some names reflect historical connections. Others derive from a particular musical mission or purpose. There are also those deriving from the physical setting in which they perform or a descriptive quality of the participants. Still others denote geographical considerations or characteristics associated with the leader.

Although choirs may have different names, each choir has one thing in common—each strives for success in achieving its purpose. Externally, although choirs may appear different in ways such as size, presentation characteristics, format, literature, and vocal characteristics, internally successful choirs are "seasoned" with just the right mix of spices. A well-curried choir is one step in achieving choral success.

INGREDIENTS:

Purpose: An understood and consistently evident and implemented rationale underlying a choir's existence—embraced, shared, and valued by leader and members, and facilitated fairly and consistently through overt and covert actions of leader.

Leader: An individual primarily responsible for facilitating purpose; actions demonstrate concern with member growth and development; consistently sensitive to personal and musical needs and concerns of members; exhibits qualities including valuing and seeking a balance between personal needs and interests with those of members.

Members: Diverse group exhibiting a wide range of individual and collective knowledge, understandings, skills, and attitudes; willing to take risks under the guidance of the leader; seek success in terms of purpose; desire to be of individual value.

Rehearsals: A laboratory where vocal sounds are experienced and explored; primary setting in which leader and members interact; place where purpose can be realized.

Music: Human qualities that can be explored, revealed, and experienced within rehearsals; item capturing and presenting potential insights into the diversity of the human condition; means through which leader and members can unite in pursuit of purpose.

Performance: Experiences where the characteristics of music and purpose are realized to the fullest for members and leader; realized primarily within rehearsals; the magnitude and depth of rehearsal experiences are shared through public performances.

Choir: Group of members with leader, organized in pursuit of a purpose; exists in a wide variety of sizes; has varying membership expectations; meets according to attaining purpose; seeks success in terms of purpose.

SERVES:

For all choirs regardless of style, shape, form, name, age, or purpose. An unlimited variety of servings are possible through combining rehearsal performances of music in different combinations. In this manner, the unique seasoning contributions of members of choir can be even more evident.

Select a leader who establishes, revisits, and reaffirms the purpose of the ensemble, who describes, analyzes, and reviews the characteristics of members, and identifies and evaluates music appropriate to the members and purpose.

Prepare members, music, and leader for a daily, weekly, or mutually agreed upon scheduled rehearsal for not less than one half hour nor more than three hours. Note: Plan ahead so that purpose is evident throughout the rehearsal.

Place members, music, and leader in rehearsal setting with low heat. Immediate and initial emphasis should be on identifying, sharing, and affirming individual members' personal and musical characteristics as important to overall choir success.

Combine choir, leader, and music in a rehearsal with increasing heat. Engage choir with music so that performances are seasoned with the unique flavor brought to the choir by each individual member. (Note: Use of members' characteristics in this manner should be done with appropriate care, as strengths may vary widely.)

Garnish each rehearsal's music continuously through the contributions of individual members of the choir. Continue to stir and mix rehearsals in this manner until the resulting "choir curry" solidifies into varied successful performances.

Transfer to public setting(s) of your choice.

Serve with programs, commentary, staging, performance variations, etc. appropriate to helping audience members connect with members' experiences in rehearsals.

Multiple servings possible. ➤●

The Wonderful World of Rounds: Incorporating Rounds into the Choral Rehearsal

Mary Kennedy

A wise mentor once told me that rounds provide "maximum effect for minimum effort." Over my many years teaching choirs of varying ages, I have discovered numerous other reasons for incorporating rounds into the choral rehearsal. Some of them are listed here:

- Rounds give younger singers training and experience with harmony and four-part singing.
- Rounds offer a strong vehicle for building choral tone.
- Rounds provide singers with practice in many languages.
- Rounds are enjoyable, easily learned, and provide an educational break from intensive work on longer repertoire.

This recipe of using rounds in the choral rehearsal will set your students up for success. Enjoy!

INGREDIENTS:
A varied selection of rounds. Selection tips.

- Select rounds in both major and minor modes, and • in a variety of meters, keys, and languages.
- Some may be composed by the masters, while others may by written by anonymous composers.
- Rounds can be found embedded in choral textbooks, published in collections, or as single *octavos*.
- Some you will have learned as a child or while camping or as a member of a scout troop.
- Consider suggestions from a list of my favorite resources.

Title	Composer/Arr./Ed.	Publisher
150 Rounds for Singing and Teaching	Bolkovac & Johnson	Boosey & Hawkes
Canons on Music	Decker	Mark Foster
King's Singers Book of Rounds, Canons, & Partsongs	King's Singers	Hal Leonard

SERVES:
Grades 4–12 and beyond.

"A round a day keeps the doctor away!" Decide to incorporate one or more rounds every week in rehearsal. Once students have learned a round, don't discard it, but continue to use it as a warm-up or as "the pause that refreshes" in the middle of a rehearsal session. The list that follows gives you a variety of ways to use rounds in your classroom.

Vocal Tone. Choose a round in Latin, e.g, "Non nobis, Domine" by Byrd or "Jubilate Deo" by Praetorius. Have students work at producing the five pure Latin vowels *ah, eh, ee, aw, oo* as they sing. The *eh* vowel will cause the most problem and so insist that they pronounce it as in the word "let."

Aural Training. Choose a round that is pentatonic, have students learn it by ear, and then challenge them to notate it rhythmically and with solfège syllables. It can even become the contest of the week.

Sight-reading. In a similar vein to aural training, rounds are wonderful tools for sight-singing practice because they are most often tonal and usually fairly short.

Minor Mode. Too many of our warm-ups and classroom songs tend to be in the major mode, but students need plenty of practice with alternate modes. So, take a minor round such as "Ah Poor Bird" (English) and teach students to sing it by eye or ear. "Ah Poor Bird" is also an excellent vehicle for teaching phrasing. Have students stand up in phrase 3 to show the high point of the song.

Singers with Limited Ranges. Rounds provide wonderful repertoire for singers with narrow ranges, i.e., adolescent boys. "French Cathedrals" (Anon., French) has only four pitches and "Summer Is A-Comin' In" (Anon., circa 1250) has a part with only two pitches.

Integration with Other Subjects. Rounds offer opportunities to interface with social studies, as rounds crop up throughout history and in many different parts of the world. So take Billings' "When Jesus Wept," for instance, and talk about the New England roots of America.

Improvising and Composing. Rounds can take on a creative character as students improvise on the basic melody and/or create alternative parts. "Viva, Viva, la Musica" by Praetorius is an excellent choice for this activity.

Compose Your Own Round. After they learn a variety of rounds, challenge your students to compose one of their own. This is a great group activity. This last suggestion is better suited for middle school and upwards. Once students have composed their rounds, then perform them all and give feedback. I guarantee they will enjoy this class. ━●

A Smorgasbord of Choral Color and Sound through Artistic Visualization

Henry Leck

For centuries choral singing from various ethnic cultures has existed in near isolation. In the European tradition, which we as Americans know best, very little effort had been made to sing outside the *bel canto* tradition. With the advent of the technological age, various cultures find themselves suddenly in an era of close proximity. For most choirs in our country, these enormous changes have led to a quandary in terms of vocal adjustment. Here is a recipe for developing new choral sounds healthfully and artistically.

INGREDIENTS:
2 heaping spoons of imagination
A pinch of humor
A full quart of imagery
1 oz. of playfulness

SERVES:
A roomful of willing singers.

If choirs sing all music in the same weight, color, and style, it is not only boring to the listener but detracts from the authenticity of the music. Often a choral program begins to resemble a loaf of sliced white bread. How do you teach a choir to sing with widely divergent character?

As a first step, it is possible to simply explore combinations of four basic elements: light, heavy, bright, and dark. By changing the conducting gesture, a choir can playfully explore singing the same passage, first light and then heavy. Even the youngest singers can then explore singing dark versus light. Then it is interesting to create combinations of weight and color together. For example, a "Russian" sound might be dark and heavy; a "Bulgarian" sound, heavy and bright; and a "madrigal" sound, light and bright. By altering these primary components, enormous variety of color can be obtained.

Oftentimes, however, simply asking for those variants is not enough. Here are several strategies for achieving variation in choral tone.

Modeling
Students are very quick at learning from a vocal model. If you are a singer and model for your choir, they will pick up your habits. Be aware of the importance of using your voice

differently for various musical styles. We tend to sing in a European style. However, if we are teaching African music, our vocal model must be much different. There may occasionally be a student who can provide a stylistic model (i.e., gospel music). If a vocal model is unavailable, consider the use of a recording. Students will pick up the character, style, and color very quickly.

Movement

The quality of singing can change dramatically when students begin to move. In many cultures, movement is an essential part of the music. When doing traditional vocalises, feel free to add playful movement. Throwing imaginary Frisbees or footballs, or stepping in time to the music and swinging arms, can produce a newfound freedom of sound. As vocalises are done, have students change the sound by showing the shape of vowels with their hands.

Imagery/Visualization

Creating a variety of sound involves more than just learning pitches and rhythms. If the student can create an internal image of a piece of music, the sound will change. Discuss the meaning of each piece of music. Come up with a series of images and encourage the students to imagine a specific scene. This works effectively if students have their eyes closed. When they have the image created in detail in the mind's eye, have them place their own image into the scene. Ask the student to imagine that scene every time the piece is started.

Another method is to ask the choir to come up with various phrases that might describe the feeling or character of the piece. When a number of phrases have been suggested, ask the students to write a phrase on the beginning of the score describing a personal description of the music. Remind your students to think this phrase before each time it is sung.

The artistic character of music can be changed when the singers are given an artistic descriptive paradigm. Examples:

- Sing as though beautiful light is pouring down upon you from a stained-glass window.
- Sing as though you are looking out over the ocean at a beautiful sunrise.
- Sing as though you are cheering the winning team at a basketball game.
- Sing as though you are at a racetrack.
- Sing as though you are looking into a newborn baby's eyes.
- Sing as though you are fearful of a storm.

Dramatic changes in vocal character can be achieved when a choir is asked to sing in a certain color.

- Sing this piece as if it were white.
- Sing this piece as if it were light yellow.
- Sing this piece as if it were red.

Gestures/Kinesthetics

Oftentimes the key to changing choral sound is right in front of you—how you use your conducting gesture. Many of us were trained in college to conduct in an imaginary box in front of us. One of the best methods for changing conducting character is to study the work of Rudolf von Laban. As a movement specialist, Laban identified the three basic efforts as being **space, weight,** and **time.** When using the two extremes of each—direct/indirect; light/heavy; quick/sustained—he identified eight combinations, each of which is then given a label: *float,* *wring*, *dab*, *flick*, *slash*, *punch*, *glide*, and *press*. By using a conducting gesture with a label, the music can take on uniqueness and a distinct character never before attained.

The true joy and excitement of artistic performance comes from an immersion in the style, character, and color of the sound. Once you have experienced it, you will never eat just white bread again. ➤●

Creating a Men's Choir in an SATB Town

Diane Loomer

Twelve years ago I was foolish (hopeful, naïve, silly) enough to try to start a high-quality men's choir in a city of only 750,000 people with six already-existing, high-grade SATB community choirs. I was also determined to never let this be an "ordinary" male choir but rather one that challenged the notion of what choirs could or could not and should or should not do. My problems were: (a) how to recruit high-caliber male singers and not offend or steal from the existing SATB choirs and/or their conductors, and (b) how to attract audiences—knowing there were only a finite number of both commodities in our relatively small community. Here's my recipe; it seemed to work.

INGREDIENTS:
A rehearsal night that fits in "between the cracks" of the existing choral schedules
A group of men whose diverse singing ability is good enough to meet the challenge of a high-quality choir

SERVES:
Any director or singers in any town or school that wishes to build a choir.
Any director or choir working to get along with other choirs in the same town.

Mixing the Ingredients
In the first few years starting out, to keep twenty-four or so men of fairly widely diverse singing abilities happy and together, divide the singers into three groups:

- **Group 1: Very Good Singers** who are so good that they are asked to pick up the music, practice on their own, come to fewer rehearsals, attend the dress rehearsal, and sing the concert.
- **Group 2: Good Singers** asked to attend all rehearsals and, hopefully, also work on their music at home.
- **Group 3: Not-as-Good Singers** required to come to all rehearsals, work on their music at home, and attend extra sessions once per week. Now here's the hook: these sessions were in my home and featured drink and freshly baked bread. (I timed it so the smell from the bread machine wafted into the piano room after about an hour and a half of note pounding). The afterglow, of course, turned into a social session, and the main problem became getting them out the front door by 11:30 so my husband (a Group 3 singer, if ever there was one) could get to bed.

The 1s enjoyed it because they could sing the marvelous male choral repertoire they had dreamed of without the "wood shedding" needed to bring the 3s up to snuff. The 2s liked it because they could do the same with some work on their own parts at home. The 3s loved it because they got to sing great music with a very good choir.

Serving the Gourmet Meal

A choral season typically consists of three popular performance times: fall, Christmas, and spring. We decided to try a system to avoid these popular times.

An ideal fall venue for a men's choir is a concert sung on Remembrance Day or Veterans Day to honor those who died in war. Choose a theme such as "Songs of War and Peace," in which song selections are associated with wars and the hope of peace, or focus on world peace, remembering absent and departed loved ones, or compassion for all who suffer. Invite veterans and their families, as well as those wanting to remember loved ones. Ours was a sell-out from the first performance and has become a fixture in the local choral calendar, with three concert times to accommodate the sell-out crowds.

Instead of Christmas, we have used two very distinct and separate types of concerts, alter-nating them depending on the energy and time of the director and choir. First is a Winter Solstice concert on or about December 21, which takes lots of work but is tremendously successful. The emphasis of the music is the solstice and return of light to the earth. It is a formula that clearly works but does not leave much time and energy for singers who also sing in other choirs. Second is "Warm and Fuzzy," using mostly familiar, more comfortable tunes and including a sing-along. In this combination the choir does not need to work as hard, leaving time and energy to sing concerts with their other choirs. We placed this as close to Christmas Eve as we dared, placed the emphasis on calmness, serenity, and quietness, and both the audience and the singers absolutely loved this one!

The spring is when to stretch your brains, ears, vocal chords, and tongues by singing difficult, erudite, classical, twenty-first century, newly composed, etc. repertoire. Because you have from early January to March or April to prepare, it gives you time to get your teeth into the "meatier" stuff. Though we originally did not count on a big audience for this concert, we indulged ourselves and called it our "serious spring concert" and the event became quite a hit with our discerning audience members.

And finally, the *really* crazy idea was to do a concert in June, when other choirs had quit for the summer. We called it Summer Solstice Serenade and sang it on summer solstice–June 21. We didn't want it to be a typical choral concert standing in straight lines in a church or hall–all wearing the same black tuxes– so we found a summer Shakespeare Festival with a tent and persuaded the organizers to let us have it on their "dark night." The first year we tried to sing fairly serious repertoire but the acoustics and the ambience soon had us doing pop, folk, show tunes, C&W, you name it, and cavorting in tails and top hats, canes, rain slickers, cowboy hats, and hockey jerseys (we are in Canada, after all). The good news is that most of the singers grew to love it after a few years. It accomplished two great things for the choir: 1) audiences who attended to have fun and laughs ended up becoming fans and attending other concerts, and 2) it attracted talented young singers to the choir.

Since its formation in 1992, the choir has now reached an international stature. We have dropped the "group" system because the choir now attracts such strong singers. We have kept our four-concerts-per-year formula but have had to increase the number of performances of each of these concerts to three, and sometimes four, to accommodate our audiences.

The choir has become recognized for its mastery of male choir repertoire, for inspiring and performing new works, and for originality in performance, all the while maintaining a high standard of excellence with a smiling willingness to try anything once. Perhaps the best result of all, however, is that the choir has now served as an example and mentor for the establishment of several more male choirs across the country. The choir is now viewed as a world-class choir in a world-class city. ➤●

Using a Modified Music Staff to Decode Pitch Notation

Alan McClung

Pitch notation can be decoded successfully when lessons are sequenced into small learning events. Turning pitch notation, which is merely a written visual prompt, into a specific pitch-related sound is a skill that all vocal students should learn to do effectively.

INGREDIENTS:
Five horizontal lines and four spaces
A (D) or a (1) to identify the location of tonic
Pitch-heads, as needed
Vertical bar lines, as needed

SERVES:
Young students as well as older students, who can sing a major scale successfully.

Preparation

This recipe for learning to read music notation uses a modified music staff that eliminates two elements normally included in the typical music clef. The modified music staff eliminates the clef sign; with no clef sign, there can be no letter names. Any piano-related pitch can be assigned to any line or any space on the modified music staff. Additionally, the modified music staff eliminates the time signature, so that all pitches are perceived to be equal in length of time.

To set up the modified music staff, draw five horizontal lines, which also creates four horizontal spaces in between. Select a line or space to serve as the location of the tonic. Designate that line or a space with a (D) or (1), depending on which of the two primary movable tonic pitch systems are used: movable-pitch syllables (*Do Di Re Ri Mi Fa Fi Sol Si La Li Ti Do Ti Te La Le Sol Se Fa Mi Me Re Ra Do*) or movable-pitch numbers (*1 # 2 # 3 4 # 5 # 6 # 7 1 7 b 6 b 5 b 4 3 b 2 b 1*). Movable pitch numbers are sung, "one, sharp, two, sharp, three, four, sharp, five, sharp, six, sharp, sev, one, sev, flat, six, flat, five, flat, four, three, flat, two, flat, one." For the raised or lowered pitches, think the call number as you sing the word "sharp" or "flat," using the monosyllabic "sev" for seven. The choice between syllables and numbers should be based on personal preference as well as a professional awareness of the primary sight-singing pitch system used in your region of the country.

Place the first pitch-head on the line or space designated D/1. Follow this pitch-head with three additional pitch-heads, each approached by diatonic step or simple leap (see example). Reinforce tonic, by making the fifth and final pitch-head of the unit a D/1. Follow the five pitch-head unit with a vertical bar line. Write five similar pitch-head units, gradually expanding the level of difficulty.

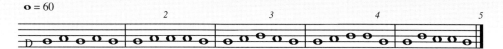

Procedure

Ask students to identify each pitch-head using the designated reading system, movable pitch syllables or movable pitch numbers. Allow students to write in the syllables or numbers when initially identifying the pitch-heads, but remove all written identification before singing. The objective is for students to learn to decode the notation, to turn notation into sound.

The teacher chooses and sings a D/1 that complements the students' comfortable singing range. Students echo-sing the D/1. Like a swinging clock pendulum, sound a clicking tactus at 60 beats per minute. There is no time signature and no numerically ordered beats, only the perception of equal length. Ask students to breathe and sing the first unit. If the unit is performed accurately, move on. Without breaking the tactus, students should breathe and sing the second unit. Continue this process throughout all composed units. Transfer this experienced knowledge to the music performed in the classroom.

Assessments

Written Identification: The student identifies each pitch with the appropriate pitch syllables or pitch numbers. The teacher provides the student with a set of pitch units. The location of the D/1 can vary.

Composition: The student composes a set of pitch units. The teacher provides the student with an empty modified music staff.

Performance: The student performs practiced pitch units on an individual basis using audio recording equipment.

Sing-at-Sight: The student sight-sings unpracticed pitch units on an individual basis using audio recording equipment.

Error Detection: The student indicates with a circle the pitches performed incorrectly. The teacher provides students with a set of notated pitch units. The teacher demonstrates each set of pitch units by singing on a neutral syllable or playing on the piano.

Pitch Dictation: The student uses pitch notation to indicate the pitches performed. The teacher demonstrates a set of pitch units by singing on a neutral syllable, playing on the piano, or singing while being supported on the piano.

How to Sauté a Fugue

Joe Miller

This recipe presents a simple process by which to teach a fugue. It could also be used for any rhythmic or theme-driven work.

INGREDIENTS:
Subject
Counter-subject or second subject in a double fugue
Stretto
Other filling (free counterpoint)
Count-singing: developed from the smallest division of the beat
(eighth note = 1&2&ti&4&; sixteenth note = 1&2&ti&4& 1&2&ti&4&)
Note: These will be written in musical notation.

SERVES:
All ages.

Part 1. Prepare the ingredients.
1. Analyze the structure (exposition, development, recapitulation) and label in the score.
2. Analyze the harmony and write the Roman numeral analysis in the score.
3. Articulate (staccato, marcato, slur, tenuto) each of the subjects/countersubjects in the score. Try to build contrast between the differing components by using contrasting articulations. Practice each until you have mastered it with count-singing. For a stronger articulation, take the "&" off of the notes that have staccato marks.
4. Identify and practice the subjects while playing the harmonic background on the piano.
5. Articulate and make stylistic decisions about other material in the fugue, such as development sections, episode transitions, bridges, pedal points, and free material. Mark dynamics that will allow the subjects to remain strong.
6. Determine the overall dynamic plan for the fugue. Make sure that this enhances the structure.

Part 2. Sauté with the ensemble.
1. Teach the primary entry of the fugue subject in unison with the correct count-singing articulation. Then, have the entire ensemble learn the subject in each part. Ask ensemble members to place a bracket or identifying mark (star, asterisk, etc.) by this

subject. This will allow them to easily see the relation of their part with the theme. When all of the entries are taught, go back and have them sing these in their own parts. Have the accompanist play the entire fugue as you ask the choir to only sing the subject. If there is stretto, teach it in the same manner during this step.

2. Teach all of the countersubjects or second subjects in the same manner. Make sure that these receive a different mark. Before adding any other notes or rhythms, rehearse these until well blended.

3. Teach all of the other material. Remember that this material is often harmonically based. You will want to work slowly and legato to ensure strong pitch. Consider using the chordal structure of the harmony as accompaniment rather than doubling the parts on the piano.

4. Combine all ingredients. Stir slowly at first to ensure good blend. Then, sauté until the music dances. Keep in mind that you always want to taste the main ingredients while not losing the spice of the other ingredients.

5. Serve with a nice Chianti.

Variations on the Teaching

Consider adding motion to the subjects and countersubjects to enhance the differences in character. For example, use large-body motions for a slower subject (painting in large strokes, swaying, stepping), and use smaller body motions for faster subjects (dabbing, playing the back of the hand like a keyboard, pulsing the body as in laughter). ➡●

Score Study: A Recipe for Success

Nina Nash-Robertson

As choral conductors, we recognize that the literature we choose for our students creates our curriculum, and each piece of music provides a unique recipe for artistic expression. Consequently, it is essential to teach and perform only the finest music available in every medium. Once we have chosen that music, we must strive endlessly to elicit the best possible performance, based upon the wishes of the composer, combined with the abilities of our students and our own educated, heartfelt response to the musical blueprint. In order to be sure we have truly prepared the best possible performance, we must always make thorough score study a first and last step. We must continually refer to the recipe—the score—if we wish to produce the greatest musical experience for our students and our audiences.

INGREDIENTS:
Choral score, colored pencils, music history and theory texts, and Internet sources

SERVES:
All choral directors.

Analysis of style, period, text, form, harmonic language, and context of the score should be completed prior to the first rehearsal, with all decisions of interpretation, tempo, and diction thoroughly marked. Colored pencils can assist this process by creating a visual shorthand, particularly in marking dynamics, cues, and structure in contrasting colors.

The first issues of score analysis involve the overall *style* of the work. What is the time period? Renaissance, baroque, classical, romantic, contemporary? What is the background of the composer and the context in which this particular work was produced? If this is folk music, what are the traditions of the area? Is the music nationalistic, celebratory, mourning, etc.? What is the instrumental involvement appropriate to music of this time and place? Is this music created for a church or temple? What is the appropriate performance practice, and how can it be expressed appropriately by this choir?

The issues of style involve extensive research. The Internet can be a great source of information, particularly regarding the works of contemporary composers. However, composers who are no longer living deserve the kind of study that musicology and ethnomusicology can provide. Every choral conductor should own, or have easy access to, books that can provide quick research regarding music history and that can point the conductor in the direction of further indepth study.

Text study is the next step in looking at a choral score. Why did the composer choose this particular text? What aspects of the text inspired the composer to make specific formal and harmonic decisions? Did the composer choose to emphasize particular words? How? Why? It is important to keep in mind that the historical and cultural context of the composition will be an essential clue to the study of a particular score. For example, though the *Ave Maria* text is clearly divided into two sections with "Jesus" creating a bridge, the compositional structures in the settings of Victoria, Mozart, Verdi, and Nystedt are quite different from one another. It is the conductor's task to find the unique stamp of each composer's setting. Virtually every text that a conductor will encounter can be studied in a similar manner. Study of the text form will invariably reveal the form of the musical setting. The conductor must also know a word-for-word, as well as a phrase-by-phrase, translation of the text. In order to understand correct syllabication, dramatic phrasing, and other related text issues, the conductor must declaim the text and have the students declaim it as a dramatic statement. Once these observations are made, the conductor will have attained clues regarding issues of diction, breathing, syllabic emphasis, etc. Note all of these observations in the score, and help the students recognize and perform them.

In many works, choice of specific **tempo** is determined by the conductor. It is important to look at the character of the text and music, the most complex rhythmic motives, and the phrase lengths in order to find an optimal tempo. Such factors as size and expertise of ensemble, acoustics of rehearsal and performance space, and relation of vocal parts to accompaniment should also be considered in making effective tempo decisions. The conductor should mark a target tempo before the first rehearsal and change, if necessary, during the course of the rehearsals. This is also a good time to note that many conductors find it helpful to use a different tempo in the first few readings than that intended for performance. It can be very helpful to rehearse fast music more slowly to pay attention to detail and to rehearse slow music more quickly to provide a feeling of phrase length and shape.

Structural analysis helps the conductor see the dramatic shape of the work, including both longer works and shorter *octavos*, and helps lead to an effective rehearsal plan. Within each major section, the music will be further divided into long phrases and subdivided into short phrases. Marking each major section with a solid line running through the full score and each phrase with a dotted line through the score can help the conductor see the logic of the piece. It will help the eye travel quickly to each section and help define the flow of musical ideas. Marking the chord structure at the beginning and end of each phrase will help define the harmonic flow. This is also an excellent stage in the process to mark all cues in the score. Once the structural analysis is complete, it can be extremely helpful to create a visual chart of the entire work.

Once the conductor has taken time to study the style, text, tempo, and structural analysis of a new work, the composer's intent begins to emerge. Now it is the task of the conductor to make decisions regarding diction, breathing, and interpretation. With these decisions clearly marked in the score, it is the conductor's challenge to read and understand the recipe provided by the composer, provide effective, inspirational rehearsals, and lead the student/singers to joyful music making. ➤

Podium Freedom

Weston Noble

At a recent interview, I was asked the question, "What is the distinguishing characteristic of a great conductor?" I probed to find the answer without a great deal of finality. Finally the very gifted interviewer smiled and said, "Weston, are you trying to say *vulnerability*?" Immediately the light went on—of course. This is *the* characteristic: the ability to be open and free.

INGREDIENTS:
Courage
Faith
Love

SERVES:
Limited only to the number of people in your presence, without restrictions.

The ability to be totally free in front of an ensemble is the goal of every conductor. Would that it might be a constant experience! For some conductors, it is a constant challenge. For others, it can vary from day to day, group to group. For a few, it is a constant ingredient, as Leonard Bernstein seemed to manifest.

Several years ago I was present at a rehearsal of the venerable Howard Swan. He stopped the rehearsal and without any hesitation said, "How many of you have ever shared yourself totally with some one else?" I was stunned. Howard, where are you going? The choir numbered about seventy. Perhaps twenty raised their hands, including myself (but only in my mind). Then he said, "How many of you have shared yourself totally twice with someone?" The number dropped quite dramatically to perhaps eight (I, in my mind again). He continued by saying, "How many of you have shared yourself three times?" Two people raised their hands (I as well again, but in my mind). Howard then said, "If you have shared yourself three times with someone, it is a miracle." (I was proud again my hand was raised, in my mind.) Dr. Swan did not share the parameters of what constituted "total sharing." Each one had to make his or her determination.

I often wonder why certain people find it more difficult to be open and free. Environment is a determining factor. Second, if a family is by nature open and communicative, this gift is encouraged in the later life of an individual; the opposite is true as well. And third, the presence or lack of the gene factor of introvert/extrovert is directly reflected in the conductor's openness and vulnerability.

The ability to share on a deep, personal level can be a challenge for anyone. I remember vividly when I first realized the need to share a portion of my "shadow" and the fear of rejection that accompanied this. Did I have the courage to be so open in such a personal a manner? Did I have the faith to believe our depth of friendship was capable of surviving such a risk? And most important of all, *would this person love me even more after my personal sharing?* Yet I decided to take the leap of faith of vulnerability, hoping the three factors of courage, faith, and love were present.

Imagine my great relief when my friend answered, "Weston, I can relate to at least 80 percent of what you just shared! I remember similar incidents in my own life. How could I think less of you?" I literally "flew" home, I felt so free! I had experienced what I now know as the bottom line of vulnerability with someone else, experiencing total acceptance from a special person in my life.

Could I take the next step, that being open and free with a music ensemble? Now many people are involved, not just one wonderful friend. The risk level is greatly enhanced. It is a different ingredient of vulnerability, not a deep personal "shadow" risk, but a more open feeling of group communication—one centered in *love*! It demands the ability to communicate *acceptance* regardless of personality characteristics and demeanors of the many people in front of you.

A healthy self-image on the part of the conductor must be nurtured—a degree of self-love that is not easily threatened. May I say this is a lifelong journey to attain such a healthy self-image, such a positive degree of self-love? And that is the *challenge* of every conductor. One can never be the recipient of too many "servings" of vulnerability with others and inner growth from reading and reflection. The *faith* to take risks with your ensemble becomes part of your daily routine!

Then the students can grow in their freedom to be vulnerable with you, the conductor. The conductor experiences even more freedom in reflecting the emotional content of each composition. And the students more readily reflect what they see in the "eye of the soul" of the conductor.

A love affair takes place. A never-ending recipe comes full circle and its depth grows and grows. Yes, lives are changed in *love*! ➤●

Voix Inspirée Soufflé: Developing the Individual Voice within the Ensemble

Granville M. Oldham, Jr.

Chefs understand the basic principle that better ingredients make better entrees and desserts. Conductors likewise know the basic principle that the better the individual singer, the better the ensemble. If your singers are amateurs that display below-to-average levels of musicianship, talent, or vocal ability, then you may need to teach the singer to sing better. This is made simple by providing opportunities for individuals to sing alone and to receive a private 30-second lesson within each rehearsal. The conductor listens to the singer then recommends techniques the singer should employ to help increase his or her vocal ability and tone.

INGREDIENTS:
3-4 individual students daily
3-6 *octavos* daily
2/3 classroom of peers
1/2 phrase to 1 whole phrase
1-1/2 minutes
1/4 of instruction
A pinch of reinforcement (season to response)
8-12 weeks of delayed gratification (very difficult to find this ingredient in normal markets; you may be required to shop at the local specialty store or you may be forced to make your own)
400-500 listeners (these are very easy to find but should be located in advance)

SERVES:
Thousands.

Preparation
While preparing a rehearsal, the conductor should include opportunities for three to four individuals to sing designated motives or phrases unaccompanied and one at a time.

Baking Time
Depends on the attitude of the baking environment (some cook faster than others)

Soufflé Container

Just as important as it is to have the appropriate dish in which to bake a soufflé, it is important to have a venue that is conducive to the musical program you have selected. After you have helped develop individual voices in the ensemble, it is necessary to make sure the performing venue is vocal friendly and allows the singers to sing without exerting tension-causing effort. Psychologically it is important to get a performance space in which you can fill the house to 80–90 percent capacity, and it needs to be congruent with the type of music you are performing. This aids inspired singing (*voix inspirée*).

Process

Beforehand, inform the choir of the main objective—their peers' ability to create an organic sound (*bel canto*) and their ability to acquiesce the skill to promote individual growth within the ensemble. It is important to note that individual lessons are for *them* and that the individual is the conduit for the entire group's learning.

To develop a general concept such as **vowel purity**, choose an appropriate warm-up/vocalise—for instance, a standard five-primary-vowel exercise. As it is repeated and modulated, point to an individual to sing alone. This way there is no time to get nervous and the exercise is very familiar. This is especially good for the more timid or less experienced singers. Without stopping and while still keeping the beat and exercise going, provide a brief suggestion, such as to increase space in the vocal tract, lift the velum, increase pharyngeal space by placing the tongue in the [e] vowel position, or manage breath better and sing on the interest of the five liters of air being used. Make sure to listen to *their* sound and suggest what *they* need to do. Teach principles of good singing: correct breath support, vowel, timbre, intensity, duration, articulation, pronunciation, or any other aspect you choose, using your choice of the Socratic method: observation, questioning the classroom peers, noting what is already correct, etc.

For a difficult motive or problematic phrase, have everyone sing that particular motive or phrase in unison to show the inherent problem. Suggest a principle that needs to be applied and have the group rehearse it together. Then have an individual sing it and prescribe what needs to be done with that specific voice to achieve beautiful singing. After instructing the individual, use reinforcement that increases the future probability of that behavior in the individual and apply what was learned to the entire classroom of peers. Often individual students will display a lower quality ingredient in front of peers, for various reasons, and may not want to share the organic product that resides therein, and so focus on qualities that will benefit their growth.

Repeat this process at least three more times, using various voice types or voice parts. It may be crucial to inform the first four students ahead of time for the success of the remaining weeks before the soufflé is placed in the concert. Individual awareness among peers allows ownership of the music and promotes self-development.

Check periodically and continually stir with gestures to solidify the consistency. To check if it is done, use a specific conducting gesture during the performance. If the skill rises, then the soufflé is done. It is extremely important to immediately smile, nod, or give a gesture of success to prevent the soufflé from falling.

Merci beaucoup. ➖●

Add More Cooks to the Kitchen: Exploring Critical Analysis and Aesthetic Perception through Expressive Listening

Christopher W. Peterson

Evaluating musical performances is a skill that all good choral conductors possess. Choirs need an accurate source of evaluation and critique to create expressive musical performances. Sometimes, however, choral singers become accustomed to relying exclusively on the conductor for musical direction and feedback. You can encourage your singers to listen more tastefully and actively through a process called **expressive listening**. Fostering expressive listeners adds more cooks to the kitchen by allowing singers to offer their musical opinions for group performance and improvement.

INGREDIENTS:
A medium helping of a musical work that is ready to refine, a small dose of time, a pinch of creativity, and a positive atmosphere for group discussion and sharing

SERVES:
A choir of intermediate to advanced singers of any age, any voicing.

Because music is an art form with great variety and variation, this recipe must be prepared in a positive, open-ended, and creative rehearsal environment. This entree will serve to refine the discerning palates of the singers and build insight into the subtleties of artistic choral performance. You can start with the following guidelines for the recipe. Like any master chef, feel free to adapt this formula to your own culinary expertise and taste.

1. The conductor decides who the expressive listeners (ELs) will be. Singers can be chosen randomly or systematically, and can range in number from one or two people to small groups or entire sections of voices. Ideally, every singer will experience the role of EL at some point in the semester. The conductor also chooses excerpts from the literature to rehearse for the duration of the recipe.
2. ELs are instructed to listen for at least one musical event that is being performed well and also to give specific feedback to improve the musical performance. On most occasions, an EL can listen from his/her position in the choir and should not sing while listening.
3. After listening to a performance of the musical excerpt by a voice section or group of sections, the ELs should raise a hand to be recognized and then offer a suggestion or comment. When desired, the conductor can randomly call on individuals to make EL comments without hands being raised.

4. The EL should listen for one of the following: correct or incorrect notes and rhythms, expressiveness of text weight, phrase shape, tone quality, clarity of diction, facial expression, intonation, or overall effect and expressiveness of the performance. It may be helpful to have a poster in clear view listing these items.

5. The EL must describe a musical element of the performance that was good, as well as one that is in need of improvement. The comment of "that was good" or "I didn't like it" must be clarified to tell the singers how to perform it differently the next time.

6. When preparing this recipe, it is important to reinforce that there is no absolute right or wrong way to perform music. Every reasonable answer from ELs must be accepted, tried, and evaluated. If you give strong disapproval of the ideas of EL students in this process, the recipe will not turn out as desired.

7. On occasion, students who are singing can also offer EL observations and can be called on by the conductor to respond and offer suggestions.

8. All singers should do their best to try the suggestions of each EL. Be sure to stress the importance of hearing and performing each suggestion. Have singers experience the way each suggestion sounds and feels in the context of the literature.

9. Every artistic performance is a choice. Allow singers to offer their musical opinions in a supportive environment. Because any group will rarely agree 100 percent on an artistic choice, the director must be clear in making his or her final choice for the performance. The conductor may further guide the ears and tastes of the singers by describing the artistic logic behind his or her final choice of musical interpretation.

Culinary Review

As you evaluate the success of this entree, you will need to pay special attention to the musical language used by the singers. They will probably mirror the kinds of comments that you, as the conductor, regularly make to the choir. As they hear more of your insights into artistic performance, and as they hear their peers describing the various musical ingredients, they will all become better at verbalizing and perceiving musical events. It really can be a lot of fun to let more cooks into your rehearsal kitchen. ➟

Singers in Motion, or Stirring Up Your Rehearsals

Rebecca Reames

Novice and experienced singers often underestimate the physical energy and total body involvement required for singing. The use of movement activities in choral rehearsals enhances and improves singers' vocal technique, music reading, performance skills, and other behaviors conducive to good singing and performance (such as focus of attention, concentration, and memorization). Although conductors are generally "in motion" during the rehearsal process, singers sometimes become a bit freeze-dried.

INGREDIENTS:

To successfully implement movement-based instruction into the music rehearsal, conductors need to

- believe in the value of movement-based instruction.
- have some or get some movement experience.
- be willing to experiment with movement strategies.

Success will motivate more kinesthetic learning opportunities when conductors see and hear the results of movement instruction on their singers' new vocal techniques and musical comprehension. Many movement layers may be stirred into the rehearsal to encourage singers in motion.

SERVES:

All choristers and conductors.

Layer 1. Physical Warm-ups

Many choral "cookbooks" and videotapes offer wonderful ideas and suggestions for incorporating physical warm-ups to prepare the body for singing. Usually the conductor just needs to commit time for this vital part of the rehearsal process. The conductor may lead these exercises or may assign a capable singer to lead the ensemble. This layer takes about 5 minutes and is most effective when performed in silence (focusing also on the breath) or with quiet music. Ideas drawn from the Alexander Technique method, yoga, tai chi, and other movement-based instruction will bring new awareness to basic movement habits and facilitate better balance, support, and coordination.

Layer 2. Vocal Warm-ups
Take a seasoned vocalise and apply appropriate movements to enhance singers' execution of that vocalise. Teach "muscle memory." For example:

1. To engage more breath energy, have singers, while singing, walk in place, make big circles with their arms, or swing arms horizontally with the beat.
2. To allow ease on higher notes, have singers, while singing a high note, do deep knee bends, bend over from the waist, or throw an imaginary hat, basketball, or Frisbee into the air.

Investigate resources but also improvise and create some of your own creations.

Layer 3. Literature and Structured Movement
Literature that you perform will inform your movement and structured dance needs. Remember, as Weston Noble says, "All music should dance!"

Early music lends itself beautifully to structured forms of dance. Singers will love singing when they understand how period dances correspond to their performance literature. Additionally you will be incorporating National Content Standards 8 & 9 into your rehearsals! (Those are: understanding relationships between music, the other arts, and disciplines outside the arts, and understanding music in relation to history and culture.) The *branle*, a basic two-step dance, is relatively easy to learn and good for processing, and the *galliard* will inform performances of sprightly 6/8 and 3/4. Investigate these dance forms and invite a dance expert into your rehearsal to teach structured dance steps to your choir.

Folk and multicultural literature also makes many connections between singing and dancing. In most world cultures, there is little or no distinction between singing and dancing. When you sing, you also move. Select literature from publishers who specialize in multicultural music and who notate the appropriate movements in the score.

Layer 4. Literature and Movement Education
You don't have to be a Dalcroze Eurhythmics specialist—trained in sequential, comprehensive rhythm education, inner hearing, and purposeful movement—to provide concrete experiences for abstract music. Such experiences allow us not to rehearse harder and longer, but to rehearse more efficiently and effectively. Apply simple movement activities to your literature when appropriate. Here are a baker's dozen activities to get your singers in motion, with or without score as appropriate in the rehearsal room:

1. Walk around the room on the quarter-note pulse as music or a drum beat is played.
2. Step the half-note pulse.
3. Walk the quarter and clap the half note (then reverse).
4. Walk the melodic rhythm.
5. Walk the first beat of every measure.
6. Walk an eight-measure phrase; change direction at phrases.
7. Walk three beats and gradually add two beats against three in the hands.
8. Men walk quarter notes while women walk half notes; switch.
9. In seated or standing positions, remaining stationary: Put hands in patty cake or stick-'em-up position, pressing partner's hands together at shoulder level with fingers facing the ceiling . . . and then move hands/arms back and forth through various duple and triple meters to experience feel of changing meters.

10. Partners tap rhythm on each other's shoulder.
11. Partners tap meter in palm of partner's hand (micro and macro beats).
12. Section stands only during fugal sections themes or motives.
13. Singers conduct patterns while singing.

Of course singers can always move into new singing formations during the rehearsal (quartets, women in front and men in back, outlining the perimeter of the room) or anything to get them moving. Stir up a multilayered rehearsal by keeping your singers in motion. Enjoy the results! ➤

Salsa Musica: Solo and Ensemble Latin-Style Improvisation

Dave Riley

Vocal improvisation can provide singers of all ages with an exciting and creative choral experience. The key to success is usually found in how the instructor feels about taking chances with the voice when the singers are allowed to experiment with new vocal sounds. Try using sounds like "bop" or "dot" for short durations and "zah" or "dah" for longer durations. Interesting vocal sounds can be created when the singer makes an effort to sound like a wind instrument such as a trumpet or saxophone, or sounds of nature such as raindrops on water, metal, or wood!.

INGREDIENTS:

Director/leader with a willingness to experiment with "layered sounds" and guided improvisation
Pianist or guitarist with ability to play in a bossa nova style (also known as a jazz samba)
Group of singers (start with ten or twelve before moving to thirty or more)
Several vocal soloists to improvise with the ensemble
Soloist with a sense of adventure and accurate time/pitch perception

SERVES:

I believe this recipe can serve up to forty hungry singers who crave to savor the delights of "Latin Flavors." Servings should follow the described format.

The guitarist or keyboard player should start by playing the following chords as a two-measure ostinato in 4/4 ||: Dmin9 /// | G7 /// :|| played in a Latin style, or bossa nova. The bossa nova style features "even" eighth notes and dotted quarter notes and is usually performed at a moderate tempo; however, bossa nova can be effective at a brighter tempo.

Singers enter on beat 1 by singing a D Dorian scale (white piano notes from D to D, or *Re* to *Re*) in whole notes. Repeat the octave D when singing the descending scale. For variety, the scale can be sung as a round with the second voices starting on D as the first voices sing the F-natural.

Once the D Dorian scale has been firmly established in all the singers' tonal memories, individuals can experiment with melodic fragments that use the notes of the D Dorian scale. As singers become more at home with the scale, the melodic fragments can become a whole 8- or 16-bar solo, using scat syllables (*bop, bah, dah*) or improvised lyrics featuring the rhythmic sounds of the ingredients (mango, guacamole, chiles, avocado, pimento, banana).

For greater variety, singers can trade two-measure solos in call-and-response. You can also add body or mouth percussive sounds for two, four, or eight beats in duration, remembering that bossa nova features the dotted quarter note followed by an eighth note with "weight" on the eighth note. It sounds like, *boom-BAH-boom.*

Salud! —●

Breath, Space, Focus: Choral Tone Supreme

James Rodde

I still remember my methods class over thirty years ago when my college choir director read a letter he had received from a high school teacher who was conducting both band and choir in a small community. "I prepare my students quite well with pitch and rhythm, and my groups perform very musically. How can it be that my band sounds so great, yet my choir, with many of the same students, sounds so awful?" My teacher then began to talk about the "supreme importance" of choral tone.

As my young career began to grow, I recognized that beautiful choral tone stemmed from healthy vocal production. Since the sound of a choir was so important to me, I became more and more of a voice teacher in my choral rehearsals. With curiosity, my ear grew to be more keenly aware of choral sounds and vocal colors. Having my singers take pride and ownership in their sound as an ensemble was something I valued. I also wanted them to feel thrilled by the physical aspects of singing. And of course, I wanted audiences to be attracted to the beauty of tone. While attending various choral conventions I listened to audience members "ooh" and "ah" about artistic choral performances, but the choir generally talked about above the others was the one that had a sound that seemed to touch people.

INGREDIENTS:
Breath
Space
Focus
Uniformity
Placement
Drama
Open Mind
Meaning

SERVES:
The young conductor beginning the journey of discovering beautiful choral sounds.
Geared for high-school-age choirs and beyond.

Consider the following concepts for your rehearsal: First, singers need to realize that they are wind instruments and, as such, need a well-maintained **breath flow** for both phonation and an artistic melodic line. The second concept is proper **space,** both in physical posture and in vowels. Try asking for a tall tone and insist that the little, more insignificant words are just as important spatially as any other word in the piece. Once reasonably satisfied with the choir's understanding of these first two concepts, ask for a **focus** to the sound. Focus refers to clarity, placement, or resonance to the tone. Having singers visualize a point to the tone or sense the spinning of sound can bring about a pleasing result. Try incorporating kinesthetic activities with the singing to enhance these three concepts: breath for tone, space for beauty, and focus for presence, interest, and carrying power.

As the old saying goes, whenever two choir directors meet to discuss choral tone, there are at least three opinions. Most would agree, however, that the **uniformity** of vowels and rhythm is crucial. Train singers, as a matter of habit, to be aurally aware of each other while they sing. Immediate improvements usually occur when a conductor simply says to a vocal or instrumental ensemble, "Listen to each other." Create a spirit of camaraderie in which singers want to unify vowels for the betterment of the whole. Unify and beautify.

Singers in the choir have varying levels of vocal color and musical skill. Some are more fluty than reedy in color, some have larger vibratos, some have very limited dynamic ranges, some have intonation issues, some have exceptional musical skills, and some have had years of private voice study while others have had none. Strategically **place** singers in various parts of the choir where they can sing most naturally and best enhance the overall sound of the ensemble. Experiment as often as necessary with various seating charts, then let your ear be your guide. You will often find that opposite voices attract. Placing a larger vibrato next to a smaller one or placing a good ear next to a weaker one often brings positive results. Try to avoid placing singers with dramatically differing heights next to each other if possible, both for visual and aural reasons.

Once satisfied with the unity of sound, help the singers grasp the **drama** of each phrase through the concepts of diction, dynamic expressiveness in the musical line, and balancing chords. Take the time to balance the color and dynamics that you want to hear. When all of the above ingredients align themselves and a magical moment occurs to your ears, the choir needs to know it. Communicate it with a verbal affirmation or perhaps just one of those genuine sparkles in the eye.

Conductors are very much products of their past experiences. Many conductors can recall the choral tone that first gave them an aesthetic thrill, perhaps something heard or felt during their high school or college years. A part of that wonder always stays in one's ear of desire, but conductors need to remain **open** to new vocal concepts, new sounds. We need to attend workshops, listen to choirs from other countries, observe a clinician working with our choir, tape and analyze our rehearsals, and take the time to sing and practice every choral line we expect our choristers to sing. Also, we should feel free to explore new vocal approaches and sounds with our choir members—after all, they're very willing and forgiving people.

Nothing helps singers put the final polish on tone color more than their desire to communicate the **meaning** of the piece being sung. Insist that every note is significant and plays a role in the unfolding of the piece. Trigger the singers' imaginations to travel to profound places. Ask choir members to "look the part" as they sing.

In the end, when we offer beautiful and meaningful vocal production, the listener is "invited in," not "sung at." And the beautiful sound created by the singers helps generate feelings of pride, unity, and emotional depth within the ensemble. Make every moment count. As Robert Shaw said, "I am amazed again and again how the mastery of successive minute technical details releases floods of spiritual understanding." Enjoy the journey.

Tasty Morsels: Using the Internet to Spice Up Your Programs

Kathleen Rodde

I am often asked, "Where do you find all of your music for women's choir?" My answer is that I find most of my music through extensive touring of countries . . . via the Internet. I have discovered and established many contacts over the years with conductors, choir members, composers, and publishers, all by Internet. With Internet access, music and compact discs from countries like Japan, Hungary, Finland, Spain, or Venezuela are just a click away.

INGREDIENTS:
A computer with Internet access, craving for new repertoire

SERVES:
All choral conductors.

One way to search the Internet is simply to type a title and/or composer into your favorite search engine. The normal result is a list of choirs that have either performed or recorded your selected piece. Many times you will discover choirs of other countries that have performed these works. From this you can pursue more information about the choirs and conductors, their past programs, CDs, publishers, and more repertoire.

For example, type in "Mary's Song" and "Knut Nystedt" into Google. In one search, the first choirs listed were Elektra and Voci Nobili. This is how I discovered Voci Nobili. I now own two of their CDs, which offer beautiful singing models for my choirs and more music to inspect and perform. When I visited Voci Nobili's Web page, I discovered a listing of their past programs. Again, more music! I then went to the next listing under "Mary's Song, Knut Nystedt" and found that the Elektra Women's Choir had recorded it on their latest Christmas CD. More music that was new to me, and they listed publisher information!

Musica International Database of Choral Music
A more specific way to search is to use *Musica International Database of Choral Music*, online at http://www.musicanet.org. There are many ways to search for music, for instance by country, composer, publisher, type of choir, or voicing. Under "publisher," there are over 1,900 entries. Just think of all of the repertoire possibilities there might be just by contacting publishers. They also have a feature called "Favorite of the Month." One month, *Ave Maria* by David MacIntyre was featured. I ordered the CD featured with this piece and the entire CD turned out to be a gem. I discovered five pieces that were new to me by buying that one CD.

Primarily A Cappella

A second specific source is Primarily A Cappella, online at http://www.singers.com/. This site is priceless for recordings, literature ideas, and contact information. Many times the featured choirs have their own Web pages with listings of even more program ideas and repertoire.

Conventions

New repertoire can be found through choral conventions, either by attending or finding the programs online or in the *Choral Journal*. Through an Internet search and e-mail, I have contacted the conductors who performed at these conventions and ordered their CDs. I have even asked for their past programs. At conventions, I look through the CDs at the exhibits. I have supplemented my last two years of programs from two CDs I found at the World Choral Symposium.

International Publishers

Finding international publishers opens up even more literature possibilities. Many of them have online catalogs and if they don't, they are more than happy to send a hard copy. Ask them for suggestions and recommendations.

Listed below are some of my most successful international publisher sources. All of these publishers are very helpful and efficient. You can normally expect an e-mail response, in English, within twenty-four hours and you can normally expect orders to arrive within two weeks. They are willing to provide inspection copies at little or no charge, and they accept credit cards.

CM Musical Editions
www.cm-ediciones.com
E-mail: cmautores@cm-ediciones.com

Pana Musica Co. Ltd.
www.panamusica.co.jp
E-mail: yoshida@panamusica.co.jp

Musikhaus Doblinger
www.doblinger.at
E-mail: chor@doblinger.at

Edition Music Contact
www.edition-music-contact.de
E-mail: mail@edition-music-contact.de

Ferrimontana
www.ferrimontana.de
E-mail: info@ferrimontana.de

Kodaly Institute
www.kodaly-inst.hu
E-mail: mhorvath@kodaly-inst.hu

Norsk Musikforlag AS
E-mail: order@musikforlaget.no

Sulasol
www.sulasol.fi
E-mail: sails@sulasol.fi

Build a Great Arch of Unimagined Bridges: Programming to Make Connections

Catherine Roma

Understanding music in its cultural context is greatly enhanced by the art of juxtaposing music from completely different sources, genres, and styles. The longing to create beauty is inherently human, though beauty is culturally defined. Comprehending the functional nature of music and the impulse behind it facilitates cross-cultural awareness.

INGREDIENTS:
Unfettered imagination
Spicy new sounds
Community awareness
Shopping in specialty, neighborhood stores
A humble leadership model
A healthy dash of risk-taking
Indigenous resource people
Cross-cultural awareness
A touch of chaos
Courage and integrity

SERVES:
This recipe will appeal to all types of choirs, especially college and community choral arts organizations: SATB, SSAA, TTBB. If we as choral conductors want to increase the gumbo in our choral groups, to build vocal community unity, this recipe is most useful to introduce both singers and audiences to new sonorities from world cultures in order to attract new members as well as broaden and diversify audiences.

The vast library of choral music often includes music from diverse populations that is from an oral cultural database. Choral conductors often want to mine this music because it speaks with elemental force and immediacy. We are attracted to music that comes from the oral tradition, from the improvisational spirit of folk and popular music. The interest by conductors and publishers in world music literature reflects a desire to make friends with strangers and awaken an emerging awareness of this rich source of indigenous wisdom.

Commission a work from a composer who presents you with an oral score. From this source, you must transcribe the work, listening over and over to decipher how you will notate music that originates from the oral tradition. The territory can be terrifying. The printed manuscript—your new recipe—may require you to abandon your relied-upon conducting pattern. As you teach from the score, your customary comfort zone, you are required to capture and interpret sounds unfamiliar to your conventional vocabulary of sounds (humms, groans, slides, smears, or dropping consonants and finding new places in your mouth for shaping a vowel).

The recipe now calls for the *roux*–the thickening ingredient of rhythmic vitality necessary in music from the Hispanic and African diaspora–transferring the music from the page to the body. Movement is integral to the music and must be understood and felt equally as part of the whole in teaching the choral context. When the choir has committed to the piece, bring in the composer. If you have worked with a published piece of music from a style or tradition other than your own background, bring in a resource person indigenous to the culture. At this point in the process, you may abandon conventional ways of operating; give up your place at the podium, step aside, turn your choir over. This is one sure recipe to bridge cultural crossroads. Ideally, interest in programming and performing world music is not just to provide variety. It facilitates understanding of cultural context and identification with another world view, and, most importantly of all, creates an inviting atmosphere that attracts new audiences and potentially new members to join your ensemble.

Sonorities you may never have imagined using with your choir are those provided by well-traveled instrumentalists in your communities, home from Brazil or Cuba, who you invite to pepper in percussion to the gumbo of ingredients already in the mix. Here knowledge of the particular folk styles and rhythmic crosscurrents may need to be left to your artistic partners.

Now that you have learned this indigenous repertoire, of course it can stand alone, or it can be programmed with musical material from vastly different sources.

Although it may seem unimaginable, here is a combination to consider. Juxtapose three pieces together that might never be found in proximity on the same program. For example, to highlight the full-voice sound of women's voices from diverse singing communities, put a Hebrides walking song such as "'Tha 'n t-uisg', tha 'n ceo air na beannan," an example of women composing rhythmic call-response songs to coordinate the felting process of making wool, as they shared their stories and lives in song, with another full-voice piece "Polegala," from Eastern Europe, a Croatian song about a young girl who cuts and harvests grass for her horses, and complete the set with "Voices from the Mountains," a piece from Appalachia about solidarity and the cry of the dying miners. Another addition to this rich sonority might be Kodaly's wordless "Mountain Nights," to diversify and enrich the choral palette. In offering this kind of programming, simultaneously performers and audience understand how singing channels courage within choral communities, courage to tell our stories and courage to act against injustice.

Programming music with imaginative juxtaposition of pieces to highlight cultural context is an exciting way to educate audiences and singers about the function and creation of cross-cultural and world music. ➤●

Bringing the Lyric to Life in Vocal Jazz

Paris Rutherford

In both solo and ensemble vocal jazz, lyric treatment is the single most important ingredient to quality performance. Whereas in classical music, vowel sound is more important strategically than the use of consonants, the opposite is true in vocal jazz. This recipe helps a serious vocal jazz ensemble and their director to realize success, while helping the individuals to grow as musicians. The performers also have fun making their music—very important these days!

INGREDIENTS:
Singers and players determined to succeed together in making great music
Vocal jazz arrangements with expressive lyrics, good rhythms, and good harmonies
Microphones and monitors that are together equalized properly
A positive approach to rehearsing

SERVES:
This recipe is designed to help vocal ensembles and soloists that perform on-mic with a live sound system, especially when the microphones are hand-held. Directors of vocal jazz ensembles can sharply economize their rehearsal time by using these ideas. Singers from middle-school age through adult benefit equally: age differences suggest difficulty levels in repertoire, not the attention to lyric.

Steps for a Delicious Lyric Treat
1. Divide the music into six- to eight-bar sections that make good lyric sense. This first step should take place before you introduce the new arrangement in vocal rehearsal.
2. Rehearse the lyrics section by section, a cappella, "in time" without the music, and at a tempo that promotes togetherness, especially with attacks and releases. Be patient with your singers at this stage, encouraging their product but reserving to the next rehearsal problem areas that are not quickly solved. This important segment of your rehearsal can be frustrating to young singers—don't spend too much time here at first. Be prepared to make it a normal rehearsal activity.
3. Identify consonants and diphthongs that are not together, especially in releases. Help the singers correct these, a bar or two at a time. In a jazz choir of twelve to sixteen singers, the singers themselves profit from listening intently to these maneuvers. This helps to build a sense of ensemble that is paramount to the success of your group.
4. Now put music to these areas, slowly at first, then at tempo. Use the piano now only with chords and time but not yet with the stylistic arrangement. Rehearse the sections, expanding to the complete first chorus of the arrangement. Record small

portions and let the singers hear themselves. The recording system does not need to be expensive and the timing of these recordings can serve as "breath marks" in the rehearsal. You will notice the change in how the singers approach their lyric.

5. Aim for a conversational presentation of the lyric as the singers become comfortable with combining lyric and melody lines. Don't let the product slip back into mere notes, words, and rhythms, once the singers become involved in the story line.
6. This is now the best time, during a rehearsal "breath mark," to ask one or two singers to share what the lyrics and music say to them personally. Get comments from others during this pause, which should not take more than two minutes.
7. Rehearse separately with the rhythm section, then add it to the group. Rhythm section members must first learn to respond to each other stylistically on an arrangement before supporting the vocals.
8. Put the entire ensemble together now and enjoy the product you have built. Your *delicious lyric treat* should be used on only one chart at a time, interspersed with other arrangements already underway. The increase in lyric sensitivity will spread to other charts you are working on as well. It's contagious!

Enjoying Your Product

By spending this time with the lyric, many intonation problems within the group are much more easily corrected when the music is added. For example, dark vowels ("ah," "oh," etc.) that tend to go flat (especially in basses and altos) are much more easily corrected when the sound of the group is conversational. That is, the sound resembles the way we converse with each other rather than the sound of music vocally placed to project to the back of a hall.

Also important is the effect that great lyric delivery has on the accompanying band. Rhythm section players (piano, bass, drums, guitar, etc.) respond very positively to vocals when the lyric is expressive and together. In the final analysis, the feeling of ensemble that emerges from the approach found in this recipe is both contagious and also unique to vocal jazz. Everyone wins, the audience is blessed, and the musicians have a great time bringing life to their music! Enjoy!

Tapas: Balanced Vocal and Musical Nourishment for Young Singers

Joanne Rutkowski

Typically, choral rehearsals follow an appetizer/main course/dessert format. The beginning of the rehearsal is comprised of a variety of warm-ups (the appetizers). The rest of rehearsal is focused on learning and fine-tuning larger music selections (the main course). Sometimes dessert is included—a performance of one very familiar selection to end rehearsal. While we still follow this format in many of our meals (and rehearsals), we are learning more about a tapas approach to eating, where smaller bites of a variety of foods are offered throughout the meal event. Perhaps this approach to rehearsals would vocally and musically nourish our young singers more appropriately.

INGREDIENTS:
A variety of activities and strategies for developing musical understanding
Music repertoire in a variety of modes and meters

SERVES:
Elementary and middle school choir members.
Students with less developed music skills and/or weak music reading skills.

Tapas are Spanish "little bites." They include a variety of small servings—typically some meat, some seafood, some vegetables, some starch, etc. Enjoying an evening of tapas allows for a great variety of food but with small portions consumed over a period of time. This approach to eating seems healthier, as a variety of foods provides more complete nutrition and the smaller portions means not eating too much! Applying this strategy to choral rehearsals would seem to also result in more balanced musical and vocal nourishment for young singers. In addition, while the whole-part-whole strategy is usually applied to the rehearsal of a piece, perhaps that strategy should be applied to the rehearsal in general.

Selecting the Repertoire
In order to apply a tapas approach to rehearsal, it is important to select repertoire that provides musical variety. While stylistic variety is usually addressed, the variety of musical content is not as likely to be considered. Is all the music "meat and potatoes": major, duple, with piano accompaniment? Or is a more balanced diet offered: other modes, other meters, other types of accompaniment or no accompaniment? Even young choral members should have a balanced musical diet.

Planning the Rehearsal

A balanced diet does not mean meat one day and vegetables the next; it is important to eat a balance every day! Therefore, once repertoire is selected, it is important to include pieces in at least two modes and two meters and with a variety of accompaniment in every rehearsal. Then organize the rehearsal for a nice flow among the repertoire. In other words, dovetail the selections. For example, if the first selection is major/duple, the next selection in the rehearsal should be minor/duple or major/triple. Change one musical element only.

Once balance is established, it's time to serve the tapas. Plan a warm-up, as you always do, to get the vocal mechanism working. But, also include an activity in the mode or meter of the first selection to be rehearsed to develop musicianship or music reading. Then it is time to rehearse the first selection. Before moving to a rehearsal of the second selection, do an activity in the mode or meter of the second piece to develop musicianship or music reading. The entire rehearsal proceeds from activity, music selection, activity, music selection, etc. The activities in between rehearsal of pieces also provide time to collect music, pass out music, etc. Since these tasks musically involve the singers, they eliminate the need to regain their attention for the next piece.

As with tapas, it is probably more logical to begin and, especially, *end* the meal with a familiar food and try the new food in the middle of the meal. The same is true for a rehearsal: Begin and end with pieces the singers have already worked on. Put that new or more difficult selection in the middle of the rehearsal.

Finally, when eating tapas you may begin with a meat selection one day but with a vegetable selection the second day. Likewise, switch the order of pieces and activities from rehearsal to rehearsal—do not always begin with a duple activity, for example. A sample menu (rehearsal) might look like the following:

1. Vocal warm-ups; duple activity; eventually half of the choir chants/reads an ostinato pattern while the rest of the choir sings the next selection.
2. Rehearse a familiar a cappella selection in major/duple.
3. Major activity: See if the choir can do a rondo; first row always sings a tonic chord, other rows sing other patterns or blocked chords.
4. Begin new selection in major/triple, with piano accompaniment.
5. Triple activity: Chant/read triple patterns, then some play on rhythm instruments; play rhythm patterns with next selection.
6. Rehearse selection introduced two weeks ago, in minor/triple, with flute accompaniment.
7. Minor activity: Students sing arpeggiated tonic, subdominant, tonic, dominant, then tonic chords in that order. Then, divide in groups that sing when the group number is shown; have a student "conductor" for this activity.
8. Sing a familiar a cappella selection in minor/duple; rehearse as needed.

A Well-Balanced Meal: Thoughts for Healthy Programming

Pearl Shangkuan

Programming for a concert, semester, or season is like planning a well-balanced meal with a variety of styles, eras, genres, textures, moods, colors, and instruments. This recipe helps to create a variety of healthy dishes for nourishment and enjoyment.

INGREDIENTS:
Music (and CDs) accumulated from growing one's own collection, music dealers, convention booths, concert programs, recommendations by colleagues, and catalog and online searches

SERVES:
Choral directors, singers, and listeners.

Step 1. Main Dish
Choose a work or works that you'd like to build the program around—something substantial (regardless of any age group or ability) that will further develop the skills of the choir members and that you would want the choir members to remember for many years to come. Choose something from the standard classical repertoire to serve as the core of the choral education and experience of your singers.

Step 2. Complementary Dishes
1. Look for a strong opener and closer. If there is an intermission, look for good before-and-after-intermission pieces.
2. Consider works from different eras, in contrasting or related keys and moods.
3. If using instruments for the main piece(s), see if one or more of those instruments can be used for other pieces in the concert, but don't overdo it.
4. Consider an international section, music that calls for different timbres, use of sign language, or body percussion. For global music, start with the *Earthsongs* catalog.
5. Use homegrown products. For living American composers, begin with Stephen Paulus, Gwyneth Walker, Libby Larsen, Morten Lauridsen, Steven Sametz, or Eric Whitacre, to name a few.
6. Program different languages—from the standard English, Latin, German, French to lesser-known musical languages like Russian, Spanish, or any Asian or African language.
7. Broaden the palette with gospel music and spirituals. Start with arrangements by

William Dawson, Moses Hogan, Paul Caldwell and Sean Ivory, Keith Hampton, and Rosephanye Powell, among others.

8. Include some easier yet well-crafted pieces.
9. Throw in a delicious dessert, something for the audience to leave humming.

Step 3. Presenting the Dishes

1. Think about the flow of the program. Place heavier pieces in the first half and then lighten up toward the end.
2. Build toward the main piece(s) and also consider how to come out of it.
3. Consider key relations from piece to piece.
4. Give an aurally balanced experience with both dissonant and consonant music, and differences in textures.
5. Put yourself in the shoes of your listeners.
6. Leave the audience wanting more, not less.

Step 4. The Utensils

1. Provide an attractive program or bulletin. For low budget, consider using an artwork by a child or chorus member.
2. Present a clean and well-set-up stage.
3. Add welcoming ushers or greeters.
4. Use a sound system that works and is double checked before the performance, as needed.

Step 5. Beverages

Consider a post-concert reception. What sort of refreshment could tie in with the program? ➡

Rehearsal Appetizers: Three Musical Skills to Tempt Your Rehearsal Tastebuds

Vijay Singh

Many choral directors consider warm-ups a mundane, repetitive, and uninspiring chore. Their choir members dutifully recite the usual array of vocalises (usually in the same patterns, tonalities, rhythms, and predictable sequence) with a passive approach and minimal musicianship. This recipe challenges the passive approach with an active one of musical multitasking in three areas of choral skill: **vocal technique, rhythmic integrity,** and **harmonic ear training**. The results are: improved flavor of musical dishes in all styles; greater rhythmic independence; improved accuracy of intervals; and improved harmonic appreciation and senses.

INGREDIENTS:
Musicianship, creativity, discipline, and positive attitudes
Preparation time: anywhere from a few minutes to weeks of practice

SERVES:
All types of choirs and applications. Customize it for jazz ensembles with more complex jazz harmonies and rhythms.

Begin with **rhythm pyramid subdivisions** on a medium-tempo "s" hiss to move the air and connect to support. Start with a measure of quarter notes, followed by a measure of eighth notes, followed by eighth-note triplets, followed by sixteenth notes, while singers walk the quarter-note pulse and conduct 4/4 time. Repeat and reverse the pyramid, going from sixteenths back to quarters.

Repeat the pyramid, but now **stagger entrances** to build independence—sopranos start, followed a measure later by basses, etc. Keep the choir walking the pulse and repeat having each section start on a different note value within the pyramid and return to their original value.

Repeat the last step but now add a pitch or assign different chord pitches (e.g., bass-root, tenor-5th, alto-3rd, sop-root) and vocalize the rhythms using your choice of counting syllables or numbers, as in 1-2-3-4, 1&2&3&4&, 1&uh 2&uh 3&uh 4&uh, 1ee&uh 2ee&uh 3ee&uh 4ee&uh, etc. Pay attention to intonation, blend, balance, and rhythmic precision. If desired, sprinkle in some dynamics, *crescendi*, or other musical spices!

Vocalize a five-tone scale in sixteenth notes at medium tempo on "Mee-ya," the first four scale degrees 1-2-3-4 on "Mee," and the last five on "ya," starting in a comfortable medium register then ascending/descending chromatically. Allow singers to make full tone and support like soloists.

Vocalize the pattern using minor tonality, and pat eighth notes on a leg as quarter notes are walked. Vocalize a five-tone scale pattern three times in a row using major, minor, and then whole-tone tonalities on vowels of your choice. Keep walking in tempo, tap eighth notes on a leg, and conduct 4/4 time with the other hand. If desired, make singers switch hands on random command without losing time/tempo! Be patient and smile a lot, affirmingly.

Vocalize triads by outlining scale degree numbers 1-3-5-3-1 or solfège syllables *Do-Mi-Sol-Mi-Do*. Ascend or descend chromatically, randomly calling for major, minor, diminished, or augmented tonalities. Be willing to hear lots of different interpretations of these triads.

Add chord extensions to triads singing scale degree numbers 1-3-5-7-5-3-1, 1-3-5-7-9-7-5-3-1, etc. Use both major and minor tonalities and chord extensions. (Very good for developing jazz ears!)

Vocalize entire scales on scale degree numbers using fingers to sign 1-2-3-4-5-6-7-8-7-6-5-4-3-2-1 or solfège hand signs *Do-Re-Mi-Fa-Sol-La-Ti-Do*. Sing the scale using solfège syllables but still signing numbers with fingers, and visa versa.

Using fingers or hands to sign stepwise, triads, or random pitches, have singers follow your creative signing—they see your fingers and respond by singing the appropriate pitch. Call out numbers or solfège syllables depending on your whim and see if singers can adjust and follow while still singing your finger signs accurately. (Are we having fun yet?)

Sing an ascending chromatic scale, returning to tonic pitch with correct interval name—minor 2nd, major 2nd, minor 3rd, major 3rd, perfect 4th, tritone, perfect 5th, etc. Then descend carefully in the same manner.

Repeat the last step, but now stagger entrances every four beats to build independence, basses followed by altos, followed by tenors, followed by sopranos.

Repeat the previous step but have each section start on a different pitch (e.g., stacked 4ths/quartal harmony, open 5ths, etc.). Have singers multitask by walking pulse, patting eighth notes, and conducting 4/4 time simultaneously. Switch hands, start on different pitches (more dissonant), and stagger as much as possible for maximum independence.

By this time, your choir will have become completely enamored with this creative approach to musical choral multitasking! Make them do this religiously every day before singing what is known as a "Recovery Piece" (I'd recommend Palestrina). The Recovery Piece acts like a refreshing sonic sorbet on the musical palette. After the cleansing process achieved by the Recovery Piece (also known in medical circles as the Sonic Enema!), you and your choir are now ready to embark on the rest of your rehearsal. Results vary, but I have found this process to be very tasty in enticing your choir's musical appetites and growth. ➔●

Teacher Behaviors that Stimulate Student Motivation

Rick Stamer

To be successful choral performers, students must be motivated to learn. Students cannot be given motivation, but they can choose to be motivated. The challenge for the choral music educator is how to stimulate student motivation. One way is for the educator to create an educational environment whereby students feel good about themselves (self-concept) and what they are accomplishing (task involvement). When this type of educational environment exists, students tend to be motivated to learn, and perform accordingly. This recipe will describe teacher behaviors that stimulate student motivation.

INGREDIENTS:
Specific teachers behaviors that serve as successful steps to stimulate student motivation. Choral music educator committed to stimulating student motivation through attention to these four aspects of the educational experience:

1. Create a nurturing environment.
2. Provide individual and group feedback.
3. Assign meaningful repertoire.
4. Present appropriate challenges.

SERVES:
This recipe serves all choir students. To stimulate student motivation, an educator may incorporate several behaviors that encourage students to become passionately involved in the choral rehearsal process.

The most effective way to motivate students to learn is to **create a nurturing environment.** Choral educators may use positive feedback to tell students how pleased they are with their efforts and encourage them to continue to work to their potential. This encouragement leads to continued efforts because it focuses on tasks accomplished rather than ego gratification. Congratulate students who have achieved significant musical accomplishments, and encourage their fellow ensemble members to congratulate them as well. Compliment the ensemble on how hard it has worked to prepare for an upcoming musical event, and use this opportunity to show that there is a direct correlation between the amount of work ethic exhibited in rehearsals and the amount of improvement in musical performance exhibited by the students. Finally, provide students with new performance opportunities, especially clinics/and noncompetitive festivals, which allow them to discover new musical information and experience success without the pressure of competition.

A second effective way to motivate students is to **provide individual and group feedback.** Each choral student needs recurring detailed explanations of their individual musical and academic progress, outlining their strengths and areas needing improvement. This assessment leads to musical independence through development of individual musical and academic skills and makes it less likely that the individual will become "lost" in the large ensemble setting. If possible, provide students with the opportunity to participate in private lesson instruction.

This individual experience can aid in the development of individual performance skills and help students become competent, independent musicians. In addition to individual assessment, students need constant feedback throughout ensemble rehearsals regarding their musical progress as a group. Group assessment leads to the development of academic and performance skills necessary for a musically fulfilling ensemble experience, which stimulates the motivation for continued participation in choral ensembles.

A third effective way to motivate students is to **assign meaningful repertoire.** Select repertoire that challenges the musical ability of students but that is attainable with effort. Achievable challenges foster student interest and motivation. Illustrate how the compositional techniques found in a new musical work relate to the compositional techniques found in a previously studied work that was of interest to the students. Help students see relationships and to transfer learning from one rehearsal situation to another, from one piece to another, and from one performance to another. Present new compositions in an exciting, enthusiastic manner that causes students to want to know more about the music. Choose repertoire that appeals to differing student interests. Facilitate learning by using strategies that allow students to recognize how information they are learning in the choral rehearsal relates to other topics of importance to them. Finally, encourage students to share information on musical subjects about which they are knowledgeable.

A final effective way to motivate students is to **present appropriate challenges.** Adjust rehearsal strategies to reflect the maturity level and musical and academic experience of the student population. One effective approach for all student populations is the whole-part-whole rehearsal strategy. To incorporate this approach, carefully select smaller sections of a difficult musical composition, rehearse the smaller sections until they are perfected, and then rehearse the entire musical composition. This approach helps students successfully master musical challenges and motivates them to tackle future impediments. As students experience the whole-part-whole approach and other learning strategies, they should be encouraged to share the most effective techniques for completing musical challenges. This helps them to discover effective strategies they may use to solve future musical problems, thereby enhancing their independent musical development.

Outcome
Without proper motivation, students will seldom reach their musical and academic potential. An effective choral music educator may positively stimulate student motivation through their actions in ensemble and individual interactions with students in a variety of ways.

To conclude, I offer the **Top Ten Ways to Stimulate Student Motivation** that highlight the most effective strategies.

1. Offer many types of ensembles so there is a place for all students.
2. Create a nurturing environment. Teach individuals.
3. Work to develop a sense of competence in students.

4. Foster student interest through teacher enthusiasm for the subject matter.
5. Carefully choose repertoire that is attainable with reasonable effort.
6. Employ rehearsal techniques that encourage students to transfer learning from one situation to another.
7. Evaluate your students regularly using both individual and group assessment.
8. Focus on task achievement rather than ego gratification.
9. Use encouragement rather than praise.
10. Attend more clinics and festivals and fewer competitions. ➤

It Only Takes a Spark . . . to Get a "Choi·r" Go·ing

Z. Randall Stroope

If you know the tune that goes to the title above (or close to it, anyway), then you probably know "Kum Ba Yah" and can still live to tell about it. There are a lot of ingredients that make up a successful choir, and the "spark" or fuel concept is one of my favorites. If you like, you can "pass it on." The spark (or idea or juncture) in a piece of music that excites the composer's creative juices is often the same spark or place that excites passion in the singers and audience members. So how do we find it and then utilize it to our advantage?

INGREDIENTS:
1 piece of quality choral literature (no generic, please)
180 lbs. (give or take 100 lbs.) of a sensitive, thoughtful director
A smattering of focused singers
A few minutes of diligent score analysis

SERVES:
The choral art and all who partake of its benefits.

The "fuel" of a piece is the section (large or small) that is the most compelling, impressionable portion—the part that engages the heart, or is the "common denominator" in the work that controls or drives the rest. It's the cornerstone. The fuel or essence of a musical work (or book, movie, musical, and so on) rarely occurs at the beginning. Can you imagine the most engaging part of a book to be the first page, or of a movie the first minute, or of a play to be in the first scene? The rest is downhill. But in fact, the "germ" or most decisive part of the work generally happens much later and is in large part subjective. The particular place "where the fire starts" will vary, but the key is that there *is* fire. Directors should ask themselves, "What sold *me* on this piece? Am I drawn emotionally to any part?" Of course, (I hope) the answer is, "Yes."

When I first taught secondary school in Denver, Colorado, I had the idea that I should start rehearsing a piece at the hardest, most difficult section. I felt *that* approach gave me the most rehearsals possible to make sure the work was learned on time. However, the first impression of the singers was often negative, and they couldn't see the forest for the trees. They had no idea of the beauty of the piece or its core interest until days later, when I finally got to it. By then, some very strong impressions had formed and not always good ones. Or, I sometimes started at the beginning—it was "a very good place to start," as the song goes in the *Sound of Music*.

Psychologists say that first impressions are strong. They linger. They trigger a multiplicity of events. The marketing community has developed strategies for years around this principle. Their goal is to immediately "sell" the product in the minds of the observers by finding common denominators with their audience and convincing them that the product is not only worthwhile, but necessary for a better life.

Bottom line: Directors should consider starting a new piece with the section that, to them, is the most compelling and makes the rest of the piece worth learning and spending countless rehearsals doing the nitty gritty. Why can't students initially understand the high point of a piece, the point that polarizes both ends, the emotional magnet that drives us to smile when opening it for rehearsal the next day? Give students the best first impression, and give them credit for very likely feeling the same draw and basic human angst that the director feels. What a common sense of intent and purpose in the rehearsal! Find the point where the "fire" starts and move from there to the other sections that are only building blocks for that moment.

What excites the composer excites the conductor.

What excites the conductor excites the choir.

What excites the choir excites the audience.

What excites the audience excites the whole community. ➤

A Children's Choir Recipe for Success

Barbara M. Tagg

Instilling a love of the choral art in the hearts of our young singers takes time, thoughtful preparation, the right ingredients, and careful attention to detail. As with any good recipe, it is a combination of ingredients that bring out wonderful flavors to tantalize the palate. The input of many ingredients and the melding of many flavors create the finished product. Below you will find a recipe to feed the soul for a lifetime of enjoyment of the choral art, beginning with our youngest artists.

INGREDIENTS:
1 trained choral conductor with artistic vision
1 capable accompanist
1 group of children who love to sing
1 rehearsal space with well-tuned piano
1 organized support staff
1 large bunch of dedicated parents and volunteers
Season to taste with additional instrumentalists (exact quantity as needed).

Add
An assortment of carefully selected choral selections of excellent quality
1 cup of skill
1 cup of challenge
1 cup of nurturing
1 cup of love of life
1 cup of inspiration
1 cup of preparation
1 cup of teaching skill
1 cup of passion for the choral art
1 cup of musicality
1 cup of proper vocal technique
1 cup of music reading skill
1 cup each of score study, theoretical analysis, and study of historical context
1 cup of excellent communication skills and creativity
Prepare in: A positive learning environment
Preparation time: Several weeks/months/years

SERVES:
Several hundred people.

Many months ahead, select repertoire and plan the concert season. Throughout the process prior to serving each concert, rehearsals should include work on vocal technique, ear training, music reading skills, musicality, collaboration, critical analysis, and mindful study and reflection. Repertoire should include something familiar, something new, and something challenging. The assortment of repertoire should include many styles of music from various historical periods and cultures, several languages, and voicings from unison to four-parts (or more), as appropriate for the age of the singers and the ability of the choir.

Daily rehearsal planning should incorporate careful structuring of the precious minutes of rehearsal time. Review of previously learned material should be balanced with the study of new material. Sequential development of skills and understandings is a must. Pacing, variety, and well-defined objectives for each rehearsal will give purposeful focus to each rehearsal and the development of artistry. Creating a positive learning environment is a key ingredient to the recipe.

Parent volunteers provide invaluable ingredients to any children's choir. Chaperoning events, assisting with fund-raising activities, and assisting the office staff with clerical tasks all contribute toward building the strong organizational structure to support the music making. In addition, the young artists see their parents' volunteerism and the inherent rewards of this service to their organization.

After appropriate sequencing of ingredients and blending, serve the final concert of joyful singing in a space worthy of the children's artistry, surrounded by a supportive audience of varying ages who understand the importance of a strong choral music education for our country's most precious resource, our children. ➡

The Perfect Blend: Every Choir Director's Dream and Goal

Axel Theimer

Major portions of books on choral techniques are devoted to explaining and promoting one or more methods to reach one of the choral field's most cherished and frequently elusive goals: to achieve choral blend. Spacing and placing of singers certainly will make a difference, as will the working on purity, special shaping, and coloring of vowels. This recipe is designed to suggest that the "perfect blending choir" can be the result of all singers achieving a minimum level of vocal efficiency—as we educate our singers to use their voices in a more efficient way, they will blend.

Blend is a result of efficient singing and not a goal in itself. The quality of the sound at the vocal folds and the overall condition of the vocal tract (short/long, wide/narrow) will always be the foundation of the sound we eventually modify to produce vowels and express emotions. Instead of covering up habitual tone quality inefficiencies by manipulating our articulators, this recipe provides ingredients that allow every singer to become vocally more efficient and thus "blend" with fellow choristers.

INGREDIENTS:

∾ *Conductor:*
1. A thorough understanding of how the voice works, especially:
    a. the importance of allowing singers (especially young singers) to sound their age and not have them manipulate their voices into sounding older than they are
    b. how to achieve a balance between breath and muscle energy at the vocal folds, which allows the voice quality—within an acceptable effort range—to be full and warm and to permit a wide range of dynamics, pitch, and emotions
2. A good model of the larynx (hopefully with some moving vocal folds), some good illustrations, and maybe a video of vocal folds in action to help singers visualize how the vocal instrument is designed and how the vocal folds function
3. A willingness to include voice exploration in every rehearsal by introducing vocalises that allow the singers to become more aware of personal vocal habits and provide suggestions that will improve their singing skills; to go beyond warm-ups.
4. No mechanical blender needed.

∾ *Singers:*
A willingness to identify vocal habits, find ways to recognize their level of efficiency, and through vocal exploration—or voice play—find answers to a more efficient and thus more expressive way to sing.

In order to achieve "the perfect blend," or a blend that is based primarily on fundamental vocal efficiency, it is essential that singers are given the opportunity to develop proper vocal habits. The first step is to allow a balance between breath-flow energy and vocal-fold adduction (closer) muscles. This balance produces a wide variety of sound qualities, all within the warm/pleasant "sound family" and all between the breathy (too much breath flow energy) sound family and the pressed and edgy (too much closer-muscle energy) sound family. Second, allow the vocal tract length and width to be relatively stable (not "held" or "put" into a certain position) and "in sync" with the fundamental frequency of the sung pitch. A stable and in-sync vocal tract avoids pinched voice qualities (vocal tract shortened, thus amplifying higher frequencies) and "woofy" voice qualities (vocal tract lengthened, thus amplifying lower frequencies).

Singers who sing with a voice quality outside these established sound quality boundaries will stick out and not blend. A very common quick-fix remedy is to have singers adjust the shape and size of various resonators (if too bright, use more lips; if too dark, show more teeth). While this will change the overall sound quality of the voice and make everyone sound relatively the same, it might not address the fact that the basic sound quality as produced at the sound source (i.e., at the vocal fold level) is the actual *cause* of the nonblending voice. This can result in every singer using the same kind of quick-fix sound controls, which limits their individual power of vocal and emotional self-expression. The more individual singers a choir has who produce a laryngeal or vocal-tract voice quality, one that moves away from the balanced sound, the less likely the ensemble will blend.

There can be many causes that make singers change their sound quality. Some of the more common ones are:

- Not hearing themselves well enough in the choir setting and thus choosing to sing louder or with a more pressed sound because they are standing next to a louder singer
- Standing too close to other singers and modifying their sound to hear themselves
- Complying with a director's suggestion to have singers "match" each other's sound
- Lack of basic voice skills due to minimal or no voice lessons

It is relatively easy to make changes in some of these areas. For instance, to solve (a), space can be added on the risers; to solve (b), place singers next to other voices. These solutions certainly eliminate many of the acoustic reasons, including the very common *battle of voices*, which often seem to create nonblending voices—and which is not fought by sopranos only! More personal space creates a sense of freedom and more room to feel like an individual. A common way singers choose to follow general suggestions to solve problem (c) is to *manipulate* their own vocal instrument (adjust length, width of vocal tract; adjust closer muscle force; adjust "formant areas") in order to match other singers' resonator sizes and surface qualities. Any blending achieved this way will encourage singers to sound like someone else, which compromises their own vocal instrument. From a singer's (and voice teacher's) point of view, this solution is not desired or desirable. Finding answers to problem (d) will rely on a solid understanding of the vocal instrument by the choir director, and requires an understanding of how to teach group lessons.

It is not necessary for singers to compromise or cover up their vocal individuality to achieve a blending choir. The more all singers move toward efficiency on the sound-quality continuum, the more the ensemble will blend. There are no quick fixes in this recipe. The basic ingredients to success are singers who receive basic vocal training, which pays more attention to the sound contributions of the larynx and vocal tract instead of adding various "spices" (quick fixes) to cover up the less-than-pleasing sound of the inefficient voice. ➤●

First Rehearsal: Setting the Tone of an Expressive "Ensemble"

Edgar Thompson

How does your new year begin? While we may feel anxious to begin a new year, we must remember that the first impression and first experiences we give to our students are important to setting the tone of what is to come. Learning to resist trying to do too much in that first hour is perhaps the hardest part. While each of us has our own way of approaching these things (and in what order) and while I have always liked to observe how others worked in these very early stages, the following was one of my favorite solutions to the first rehearsal.

INGREDIENTS:
Unison art song
Primary concepts of ensemble singing, expression, and phrasing

SERVES:
High school or collegiate situations mostly, although it is readily adaptable to junior high as well as community choirs.

Introduction
Center on three things in the first rehearsal: (a) ensure that some sort of important musical experience culminates; (b) establish in the minds of the students the fundamental elements considered to be important in ensemble singing; and (c) introduce the shaping of phrases and its importance to a truly musical performance. Ultimately, of course, find out just how this new group of singers sounds together and have them feel the joy of their combined sounds. The disciplines of rhythm and intonation can come later.

Exposition
To begin the first rehearsal, consider the choir as a two-section ensemble, male and female instead of soprano, alto, tenor, and bass sections. A solo art song sung unison serves to introduce primary concepts, selected such that the notes are relatively easy to pick up and that the tessitura is in a range that can readily be sung *tutti*. In unison, phrasing occurs simultaneously in all voices thus simplifying the explanations regarding the elements of expression. Furthermore, the concepts of ensemble are most easily explained, evaluated, and achieved in these early stages through unison singing. Finally the choice of this level of literature indicates to the choir the quality of the literature that would soon follow. There are virtually

unlimited choices available. One of my favorites was Brahms' *Wie Melodien* for its wonderfully graceful phrases and lovely text.

Development: Ensemble Singing

In auditions, among other qualities, I distinguish the quality of the individual voices as either **foundation**, a type that contributes largely to the choir's underlying sonority, or **coloristic**, those who have a distinct effect on the timbre. The latter are generally more mature and may have some private training. I regard both to be equal in importance with the relative balance, often by happenstance rather than by any preconceived notion of the ratio of one to the other. What is important is how they work together. And it is this learning to work together that is the goal of the first rehearsal.

To begin, choose a foundation voice whose quality you know well and whom you know has the confidence to demonstrate a melodic line using a fine vocal production that works well in ensemble. The concept of "ensemble" encompasses many things, so without necessarily defining the term, ask the singers to think in terms of an ensemble rather than a solo experience. Tell them that all voices must be heard but none should dominate, other than for coloristic reasons, as the literature may require. The idea is to stress the equal importance of all individual contributions.

Ask the demonstration singer to perform the first phrase or two of the art song, even several times, pointing out the elements of phrasing that we will be discussing as we go along. Stress that to be truly musical, the ability to phrase comes from each individual understanding the principles of expressive singing and that the phrase must arise out of the music in an organic way and not sound "pasted on" just because the director has said it must be done that way. Stress that this will be realized later as we work in parts where the phrases in individual lines may not occur simultaneously as in unison.

Ask other voices to join in one at a time, trying to match the others as closely as they can without unduly sacrificing their individual quality, and, for those not yet singing, to sense how the two, then three, then four, etc., voices work together. Matching for the sake of ensemble, tell them, includes matching in pitch, volume, and vowel concept (the details of which, along with stressing rhythmic precision, are saved for a later time).

This process is repeated for both men's and women's voices. Work through as much of the song as possible, at times beginning this matching process over again in later phrases and using a second or third voice as the example, as time allows.

Recapitulation

Generally you can get through all of this in the space of an hour and conclude by singing through the entire song with accompaniment at least once, or several times while alternating appropriate phrases or verses between the male and female voices. Work on this song periodically over the next days and weeks, trying to feel it as a solo performer would. Eventually the piece becomes a showcase of the basic sound of the choir, and the singers will have learned a great deal about expression and interpretation as well as ensemble. With this much invested in the song I always included it on our first concert of the year.

Coda: Whose Choir Is It?

An ironic commentary on the importance of the conductor is succinctly noted in a cartoon I framed and hung on the wall of my office. It shows a street musician standing on a small podium with his upturned hat on the ground in front of him. In his right hand is a baton and his arms are raised in the position just before a preparatory beat. He is alone except for a curious passerby who has stopped to look at him. In the cartoon's caption the musician asks the stranger, "Would you like me to conduct one of your favorites?"

People sing in choirs for many different reasons, as we all know, but I know of no one who sings in a choir for the gratification of the conductor's ego. We need to recognize that we are dependent upon people who come to us seeking an experience that fulfills needs of one kind or another. Every person is important and it is an awesome responsibility for us to assume. Consistent use of the personal pronoun in place of a more inclusive "we" implicitly bestows choir ownership on the conductor. My most respected mentors held to a philosophy that the singers own the choir and we are but the stewards of the organization, with only temporary custody. A seasoned instrumentalist once spoke to me of an experience she had playing with Robert Shaw. I believe her words express the concept as well as any: "Without having to say it, he invited us to come in and make music *with* him, not *for* him." ➤●

Do Not Be Deflected from Your Course

Robert Ward

If it is true that it takes a village to raise a child, it is equally true that it takes a community to nurture a teacher—especially a new teacher. The issues that accompany teaching are challenging and sometimes overwhelming. New teachers need to know that they are not alone and that what they are experiencing is a normal part of the maturation process. And this is where senior members of the community play a vital role.

INGREDIENTS:

A safe meeting place (preferably away from school), the courage to share stories and vulnerabilities, and the willingness to listen with compassion and empathy

SERVES:

Teachers in the first five years of their teaching careers and veteran teachers who seek to nurture and mentor the next generation.

Two years ago I met a woman (I'll call her Tracey) who was about to embark on her first year as a public school music teacher. I gave her my business card and asked her to write to me and describe her first few months in the classroom. The first e-mail arrived in September, filled with everything I expected. I quickly wrote back and encouraged her to not be deflected from her course and I told her that I believed in her as a person and as a teacher. Her second e-mail arrived in early November and it, unlike the first, caused me concern. In this second e-mail she wrote the following: "I still wake up everyday and say, 'Oh, God, I can't do this again today. How am I going to make it through this day?' Maybe feeling like this means I'm not cut out for this. You know, sometimes I wish I didn't feel so much. I think that I have to get the message across to every kid or I'm some sort of failure."

The first issue here is that of saving the world. Where in our process of training music teachers do we communicate to them that they have to reach every student? I know that early in my career I felt that way, and to this day, when a singer elects not to return for another semester, these same feelings can emerge. Lately I have wondered why music teachers assume a greater burden than physicians. Medical students are taught that some illnesses are beyond a physician's power to heal. Similarly, we senior-level teachers need to do a better job of convincing young teachers that they need not carry the burden of believing that they can, or should, be able to reach all students. Such a belief system is not realistic, it is not healthy, and it will ultimately drive talented teachers from the classroom.

Now the fact that Tracey has the capacity to feel and care is exactly why we want her in the classroom. But the flip side of this is that she tends to lose heart because teaching, by its very definition, is a daily exercise in vulnerability. Teachers teach about things they care about, and what we care about defines who we are. To have our subject matter dismissed or diminished by students, their parents, or an unenlightened administrator causes our sense of self to be in conflict. In his book *The Courage to Teach*, author Parker Palmer writes that, "unlike many professions, teaching is always done at the intersection of personal and private life." We have all seen teachers who walk into a classroom and immediately distance themselves from the students and the subject matter. But gifted teachers don't walk into a classroom and immediately tune out their internal world. In fact it's quite the opposite. As teachers we share our thoughts, our stories, and our passion for music and the arts. And it is this very act of sharing that makes us vulnerable.

As a novice teacher I remember thinking that the arrows of indifference and judgment were sharp and their capacity for inflicting pain enormous. Twenty years into my teaching career I find that those arrows still fly and that their tips are still sharp. But now the pain passes more quickly, and I am aware that the wounds are not fatal. Part of my longevity in this profession is due to veteran teachers who elected to share their stories with me. Sharing stories is a special gift because they remind us that we are not alone. Hearing that others have endured the same arrows and that others experience crises of faith lends the perspective that arrows are a natural part of being vulnerable in a public arena.

I think part of the problem stems from the fact that as children we all read the same books, and they all ended with the same final phrase: ". . . and they lived happily ever after." In his best-selling book, *The Road Less Traveled*, author M. Scott Peck makes the statement that one must fall out of love before real loving can begin. Until we are able to lose the fantasy of who or what someone or something might be we will never be able to live comfortably and successfully. Like young couples who discover that marriage is much more work than they imagined, so young teachers must work through their idealized reality of day-to-day teaching. And as the transition from idealization to realization takes place, both the young married couple and the young teacher depend on the support of a community.

For teachers, that community might be ACDA, MENC, or whatever teacher's organization exists in your community or district. I encourage veteran teachers to use your position in the professional community to mentor the newest members of the community. Talk to them, listen to their stories, and share your own. Let them know they are welcome and that when their resolve becomes unsteady there are people who can help so that they will not be deflected from their course.

The Oochy-Goo Express: A Recipe for Relaxed Breathing

Guy B. Webb

The purpose of this recipe is to enable singers to begin a tone without tension and to improve the tone of the choir. The key to a good attack depends on the quality of the intake breath *senza* tension. We breathe normally sixteen to eighteen times a minute. A runner breathes over a hundred times a minute! A Meditationalist, six times a minute. This should be the singer's breath also, and our first rehearsals can well achieve this important principle until the action is involuntary. The following is a recipe for assuring a good choral attack.

INGREDIENTS:
1 end of a phrase
1 "oo" vowel formation
1 slightly audible and deeply felt "ooch"
1 very relaxed larynx position
1 very deep and open column of air down to the toes
Pop eyes
Hollow cheeks
1 soft palate that is flexible and willing to achieve a high, domed position
1 very slow (5-second) total relaxation of all throat muscles
1 very long (5-second) filling up of the diaphragmatic area
A flow of breath through the vocal cords that leads to the next intonation/phrase

SERVES:
All choirs.

Begin with a complete relaxation of the air column following the cut-off of the previous note or phrase. To experience this relaxation of the breathing mechanism, direct the choir to maintain the last vowel formation without any change or tension whatsoever on the cut-off, with *no lip movement*. Before forming the vowel for the next attack, have the choir for a brief moment experience *no intake breath*. Nothing! After a 5-second pause when total relaxation is experienced, audibly emote a soft, low "ooch" from the very bottom of the breathing mechanism, with simultaneous pop eyes, hollow cheeks, and a relaxed larynx.

The "ooch" will enable the singers to sense the depth of the air column—almost to the toes! This low, relaxed sensation—followed by a very slow intake of breath—will enable the breath to flow without tension through the coming together of the vocal cords as the new vowel is formed. This Bernoulli effect–which can be demonstrated by blowing between two pieces of paper and finding that that the papers are drawn together–is essential to a good attack, and the result is a tone placed on top of the air column. This is a very precious sensation and important to the development of what might be called "a moving tone." It is also the best way to assure that the next attack is precise and together. Listen carefully to attacks after a breath; they can be a major problem without this breath movement into the start of the new tone.

Take plenty of time to replenish the air supply. Remember the Meditationalist breath of six breaths a minute–5-second inhalation and 5-second exhalation? Then, through this relaxation, start the tonal attack with this same sensation. Each singer will experience a greatly improved tone. Most important, the often nasty high-tongue vowels–"ee," "ih," "eh," and "ae"–will not be so spread and thin. It's a great technique to be experienced in vocalization or at any time in a song that the conductor chooses–in rehearsal, of course. Contrary to this feeling of relaxation that the "ooch" provides is the high, audible stuff that so many cultivate under the guise of "getting a good attack." Good singers never breathe audibly or let you see any heaving of the upper chest activity or throat tension. After all, a good attack depends on the clarity of the ictus in the conductor's pattern to achieve an exact moment of beginning the tone–the attack. The conductor has an important role to play in freeing the choir from any tension on the intake breath.

The start of a phrase is very much like the starting up of the old steam locomotives. I remember as a kid watching trains as they stopped to take on water in our small Missouri town. With the task of pulling a long row of cars, they backed up first! The cars of the train were literally squeezed together, taking up the space between the loose couplings, and therefore the engine had only to overcome the inertia of one car at a time–not the whole train! Likewise, the singer need not impel the entire phrase, only the very first note, and the rest of the "cars" will follow. The relaxation caused by the "ooch" sensation will enable this leading of the tone by the breath to happen, very much as a locomotive pulls a train. The choir will gain a more beautiful tone quality, and the attack will be more coordinated and precise. It's called the "Oochy-Goo Express!"

Growing Pains: The Trials, Tribulations, and Eventual Success of a Recovering Perfectionist

Susan Williamson

I think some of the greatest tips about successful choral experiences may be found in the transformation of our darkest moments, for our development as choral educators is shaped by both positive and negative experiences. While our confidence is built from the moments in which we are wildly successful, the moments we wish never happened have much to tell us—these moments are waiting to be probed, explored, and turned into gold. The following essay is a narrative tale describing a period of personal artistic darkness and how one choir, a beautiful *Ave Maria*, and stillness transformed me.

INGREDIENTS:

A choral director of any age or experience who has visions of the "perfect" choral sound instilled in his/her head, a choir of truthful singers, a piece of beautiful music, a car, towering trees, and a period of quiet, thoughtful reflection

SERVES:

Nearly every graduate of a music school! Applicable to each director from elementary choir to the elite community or professional ensemble. Serve with a healthy dose of humble pie as a side dish.

I left the rehearsal feeling ineffective and dejected. Just minutes before, eighty selected middle school girls from Seattle and surrounding suburbs stood before me rehearsing the Saint-Saens *Ave Maria*. For most of the rehearsal, the girls had worked hard to accomplish what I'd asked of them. They sang with resonant tone and accurate pitch. They performed rhythms with a gentle precision appropriate for the delicacy of the piece. They achieved the legato line and lengthy phrasing I was asking for. Others would probably have been pleased with the rehearsal. But, I, ever the perfectionist, was not.

We were preparing our holiday concert repertoire for a premiere performance in the newly opened Benaroya Hall—home of the Seattle Symphony. The hall was being lauded as one of the most acoustically perfect performance venues in the world. Yes, the acoustics of the hall gave freedom to the most delicate nuances of the oboe and English horn; however, in my mind, the perfectly hallowed halls would amplify every inaccurate pitch, every un-resonant uttering of the adolescent girls I conducted.

The following weeks brought an increasing feeling of nervous inadequacy. I wondered if I was "good enough" to do the job. I wondered what would happen if our pieces fell apart during the concert. I fretted. I stewed. And, I used every rehearsal technique I knew to control my intended musical outcomes. I spent hours preparing each rehearsal—reviewing the parts I had already memorized as if, by reviewing them more, my singers would magically begin to match the flawlessly created soundtrack I had formulated in my head. Some of the singers sensed my apprehension. A few students asked how stressed I was about the upcoming concert. I replied honestly that the stakes were very high and that I felt very nervous. They seemed quietly disappointed in my response.

One day, overwhelmed by stress, I slammed down the piano cover and headed to the mountains. Past the traffic and density of the city, I drove up into a world where the cedars towered about the freeway and quiet seemed to overtake the traffic. I followed a narrow road that ended by a small lake surrounded by thick woods and dense undergrowth. Sitting by the lake, I verbally expressed my dismay and poured out my frustration to God. I shouted. I cried. And I stomped around like a wild woman with no one watching. "Why isn't this coming together?" I screamed, followed by, "What shall I do? It's not RIGHT!" And when I'd poured out my frustration for nearly twenty minutes, I finally became quiet.

After an extended period of silence, there, in the beauty of nature, in the raw power of a palette of greens and browns, of wildlife and fowl, I remembered what was truly important. I recalled the faces of my singers, who had tried so hard to please me and who must have felt let down by my lack of pleasure in their music making. I realized how much my drive toward the perfect performance had stunted my own joy. And I recognized that what I had perceived as a positive attribute, attention to detail, was my own need for control and success gone awry. My perfectionism had not only limited my own musical joy, it had inhibited the natural artistry of the choir. In his book *The Musician's Soul*, James Jordan reminds choral educators that "at the very least, this can hinder the music making of the ensemble" (Chicago: GIA, 1999, p. 110). In trying so hard to please me, my singers had become too focused on the technique of the music, rather than on its free, natural, and soulful expression.

I am pleased to report that after weeks of self-torture, the quiet revelations of the wilderness stayed with me. The night of the concert, I consciously chose not to focus on musical technique (the proper cut-offs, the perfect conducting gesture). Instead, I focused on the faces of the singers and the artistry they were pouring forth. And a wonderful thing happened. The reduction of my screaming inner critic allowed my attention to focus where it should have been all along—on the expression of beauty and on the connection that I felt with the choir. In truth, I remember that performance as a deeply aesthetic experience—a time when my heart opened and the music poured forth from the souls of these young girls. It was not perfect, but it was filled with beautiful moments that would not have been born had I continued my intense drive for the perfect *Ave Maria*.

I still struggle with perfectionistic tendencies. I still listen to the tapes in my head, which feature exquisitely sung renditions of whatever the choir is working on! But, I know now that I want to carefully choose how the tapes are utilized—for enjoyment or frustration. And in the end, I realize that great gifts of learning and growth sometimes come disguised in ugly packages of painful moments, moments where we are called to a deeper understanding of ourselves and the elements of choral music we treasure—of beauty, of sacred connection, and of letting go of control to something greater than ourselves. ➥

Savories, Spices, and Sweets: Programming Considerations in an Increasingly Diverse Culture

Judith Willoughby

An unprecedented explosion of excellent published choral repertoire representing diverse cultures has provided choral conductors significant opportunities to foster understanding in an increasingly complex world, through ensemble singing, while also developing core choral skills. How each director balances the musical and developmental needs of his or her choral ensembles with the demands of the job, while also framing repertoire choices within an authentic context, is the challenge to be met as each conductor chooses repertoire.

INGREDIENTS:

Mindful reflection by the conductor should include answers to the following questions:

- What musical skills should be developed within my chorus(es)?
- What is the realistic timeline for developing those skills?
- What repertoire will best develop those skills?
- What nationalities, races, and ethnicities are represented by the singers in my chorus(es)?
- What are the demographics of the greater community within which I live and work? What nationalities, races, and ethnicities do they represent?
- Are there visible members of my community representing diverse cultures (i.e., educators, merchants, worship communities, etc.) that could help identify authentic cultural resources within my community?
- How do I achieve a programming balance between the old choral chestnuts that have stood the test of time and the performance of world musics?

Concurrent with the questions posed above, an ever-expanding base of knowledge by the conductor should include an awareness of the questions to ask and an evolving group of answers to the following questions:

- What online, print resources, technological resources (music publishers, articles, DVDs, CD ROMs, etc.) provide accessible and/or authentic information on repertoire and performance practice?
- How do I learn to teach and lead performances of choral music outside of my cultural traditions?
- What is practical to tackle, given the parameters of time, resources, and skill level of my chorus(es)?

- What is negotiable and flexible in providing a collaborative, authentic performance experience for the chorus, audience, and community? Is the very nature of this question, in this particular situation, mutually inclusive or exclusive?
- What outcomes for my chorus and my community are desired, over time? How do these outcomes change as the chorus explores more deeply the musics of other cultures?

SERVES:
Choral conductors working in universities, public and private schools, worship, community, and professional settings.

Start small. Mighty oaks from little acorns grow. Identify a single piece from another cultural tradition that taps into universal feelings and recognizable human experiences that cut across cultures. Contextualize the music by selecting a choral score with ample notes and directions that explain the cultural history and also provide pronunciation guides and performance CDs and/or DVDs. Solicit insight and feedback from your identified authentic resource during the initial study and preparation to present this work to your chorus. Continue the dialogue at different times during the rehearsal process, particularly as one moves closer to the actual performance. Begin a dialogue with a conductor that you know has successfully bridged cultures through choral performances representing musics of diverse cultures.

Build a partnership with members of the local community represented by your repertoire choice. This could mean many things, depending upon one's community. A chorus from that community might join with your chorus for one song, a portion of the program, or the whole concert. A reception might be held featuring the food and culture of that community. Someone with contextual knowledge of the origins and practice of the piece to be performed could visit rehearsals to assist with language or to share the cultural context. Perhaps that person could speak to the audience briefly about the piece in a preconcert talk or in an audience dialogue following the actual performance of the work at the conclusion of the concert. Shared or cross promotions could be held with multiple performances in different communities. Interest your local media in the story and chronicle your chorus's exploration of the work on your organization's Web site. The possibilities are endless and are usually driven by the varied and often untapped resources in each community.

Be sensitive in the overall concert programming so that all repertoire—core western European choral canon and world musics—are given parity by their placement in the program, the mood and sentiment of the text, the vocal demands, etc. Do not assume that the loud, fast, world music or ethnic selection should always end the program. Explore ways to group selections thematically to enhance and best present each aspect of your program.

Have an overarching plan that might be several years in scope for the exploration of new world music. One cannot be all things to all people simultaneously. But a deliberate attention, over time, to the beauty and wealth of interesting choral music, paired with those works from the historical canon of literature that many choral musicians know and love, provides a refreshing, informative, and stimulating experience for chorister, conductor, and audience alike—an experience that encompasses the savory, spice, and sweet that pique our palettes in delightful ways. ➡

Making a Section Rehearsal Successful

Tom Wine

Section rehearsals are unique opportunities to allow singers of the same part to work in a concentrated manner to take ownership of their music. In a full rehearsal, singers only get limited time on their notes, even though directors need to keep the entire group involved as much as possible. It is important to balance rehearsal time during a section rehearsal. Singers need to sing some longer sections of the music to conceptualize what the director is doing and get an overview of the new piece of music. They also need multiple repetitions to drill short sections and respond quickly.

INGREDIENTS:

A multisection choir, practice rooms for each section of the choir, a piano, a leader for each section of the choir

A lesson plan with an overall objective. Example: "Today we want to get through measure ___ on page ___."

A marked score indicating where you think singers will have difficulty singing a particular passage. This will also translate well to a lesson plan that prepares for specific problems.

Secondary objectives for each time a section of music is repeated. Be sure singers move beyond the learning of pitches and exhibit some musical growth. Example: "Try that again and watch your dynamics," "More attention to the text," Or "Clean up the final consonants."

Options for performing in alternate positions. Example: "Get in a circle" or "Gather around the piano."

SERVES:

All choir students.

Begin by helping the group develop a sense of the pitch or tonality for the piece they will be singing. The main focus of any section rehearsal should be pitches and rhythms. However, before "spoon feeding" every note, let the group members work out some problems themselves. Directors are often surprised by how much singers can fix on their own. Sing the same section twice, giving the singers a basic focus for each repetition. Example: "Watch your rhythm" or "Be careful of the skip in measure ___." In other words, tell them *why* you are repeating something.

An effective rehearsal technique is to have the singers raise their hands whenever they know they have missed a note. This helps determine how much polishing should be done with each activity before moving on to the next section of music and whether to stop the whole choir for one person's mistake. An important concern is if the whole section is wrong and no one in the section raises his or her hand!

Plan in a section rehearsal to work unaccompanied. Don't rely on the piano for every pitch correction. Try using the piano to add the bass line or help the singers hear their part in relation to the top voice. Don't always go back to the piano for pitches. Trust the singers. Give them more ownership of the score.

As directors, we frequently focus so much on the music and the score that we forget to evaluate the components that could have a dramatic effect on the group performance. For instance, keep monitoring the group posture. Be sensitive to the group's physical involvement and alternate seated and standing posture. Move around the room. Try to listen to individual voices, offer group suggestions, and put reminders on the board. Be sensitive to director pacing and sequencing. Let the group sing more and make the director talk less.

Practice using solfège or neutral syllables and transitioning to text. Slower tempo is usually helpful to introduce notes, but don't forget to return to performance tempo. Be honest in your evaluation. Singers know when they need work. Tell them what sounded good.

Chef Advisory

Be careful with the use of "I" statements. Example: "What I want to work on . . ." This implies that the rehearsal is for the conductor and not the singers.

Beware of the word "quickly." By saying this one word, it implies that you want to "rush" through this activity to get to something better. Either make this a meaningful activity or skip it in the rehearsal.

Plan carefully when singers are asked to speak parts in rhythm. Get a speaking activity to transfer to dynamics and tone color. Try to make speaking an energized activity. Get singers to shape vowels or explore dynamics, something to get them out of a monotone speech pattern.

Section rehearsals might be the time to get away from a traditional conducting pattern. You might "keep the beat" with snaps or claps. Think about nontraditional conducting gestures you and the singers might use to reinforce specific concepts. Plan for kinesthetic teaching!

Think carefully before asking the singers, "Do you have any problems?" The implication of this question is to give control of the rehearsal to the singers in the ensemble who choose to respond. If this is an evaluation technique to determine if singers can recognize their errors, then it can be very effective. If it is because you, the conductor, don't know what to do next, then it leaves open several possible negative rehearsal scenarios.

Serving Up the Text

John Yarrington

Because we are always rushed and there never seems to be enough time to accomplish what is needed in rehearsal, we are tempted to go for the "right notes" at the expense of the spirit and life of the music. We fall into what Alice Parker calls the "reading syndrome"—the "let's learn the notes and rhythms and let the conductor supply the interpretation." Dear reader, there is a better way.

INGREDIENTS:
Choose a meaty text, one that uses words with care and precision, set to music that does not violate the basics of prosody and word accentuation.
Add intelligent singers who are willing to speak lovingly, meaningfully, musically.
Stir in the music after the text has been assimilated and *voilà*: a wonderful treat.

SERVES:
Any age group wishing to do something more than sing the correct pitches and rhythms, and willing to try textual inflection and nuance.

It is always appropriate, yea necessary, to work on "choral hygiene"—that is, vowels, conso-nants, breath connection, agility, range, dynamics, articulation, mood, color, and nuance, in order to have a good performance. Embracing this philosophy, our rehearsals can be well paced, lively, and energetic, beginning with solid tonal concepts in the warm-up and continu-ing through a variety of musical styles and difficulty.

How one begins a piece is, I believe, crucial. Often playing through as the singers listen or using a recording is valuable, particularly with less accomplished singers. I know there are those who don't think recordings should be used at all, but I think the singers welcome the chance to hear how the piece goes. You should then develop your own interpretation based on your musical ideas and standards and the skill level of your group.

I almost never have singers read through a piece, which is interesting and challenging for the good readers, but frustrating for many. I almost always start with the text, speaking and listen-ing to word shapes, meaning, rise and fall, and looking for phrase destinations. This should not be viewed by the choir as punishment. Rather, it immediately focuses on text meaning. To "pound out" the correct notes and then add correct rhythms and pitches is nonsense. To quote Alice Parker:

> It is a misunderstanding to see the page as a basic source of information which, if fol-lowed exactly, will yield a usable product. Imagine a recipe, followed exactly with no

care for the freshness or flavor of the ingredients. To improve the product, one can't just add a few seasonings—one has to go back to the beginning with new ingredients and a new focus: flavor FIRST, not last. ("The Backwards Method," *Melodious Accord 2*, June 1995, p. 1.)

Often, I introduce an anthem by asking the singers to read the text aloud, not in the rhythm of the music, but in the rhythm, color, and sound of the text itself. Reading again, one listens for the variety of enunciation, color, and nuance possible and exaggerates the differences. Reading a third time allows the enjoyment of vowels and consonants as they feel in the throat. My rule of thumb is: speak for meaning, pause for importance, linger to love. Parker also said in her article:

> In music based on text, the "flavor" begins with the text. Not just sacred or secular, or what it "means" but how it feels in the throat (vowels and consonants), and how it flows and is captivated on the tongue of a loving reader.

Though this may seem slow, we gain in the long run. Most of our singers have trouble handling text and tune at the same time. When we approach the music by the "reading syndrome" (get the right notes, put in the phrasing, enunciation, and color later) we most often get a sameness of sound and articulation that I characterize as the "Holy, Holy, Holy" sound—that is, singing everything in four parts, homophonically, fairly square, and flat-footed musically.

After beginning with text, I deal with the music in various ways. If the tune is prominent, then we all learn the tune, with consummate inflection and nuance. Singing on a neutral syllable is cleansing. If the setting is polyphonic, speaking in rhythm (again, musically) helps everyone hear the togetherness of the piece. Rhythm does create blend. Asking two parts at a time to sing while the others lightly speak, reversing this procedure, then putting the whole back together, is another approach. Sectionals are helpful but only if the musical aspects are well understood. Learning the correct notes and rhythms without context is paramount to musical disaster.

Your own voice is your best model. You sing with the shape, nuance, tone, destination, and articulation you wish, then listen to "them." Never sing *with* them unless you don't want to *hear* what "they" are producing. Then, there is conducting, which is the subject for another sermon. We sway, grunt, groan, clap, snap, and then are surprised when our folks don't approach a musical product. In conducting, I believe that less is more.

We can develop in our singers their ability to recognize the overall form and shape of a piece, to love the poetry, mastering the vocal ability to use the appropriate sound, sensitive to all of the flavor and sheer fun of vocal performance. ➡

Easy-Bake Score Study: A Simple Recipe for All Occasions

Steven M. Zielke

Most score study recipes are too complex, require too much time, and make assumptions about "cooking skills" that are unreasonable for many choral directors. As a result, too often we rely on the equivalent of the "fast-food" approach, picking up details about the music as we go along, often surprised and embarrassed in the rehearsal. This score-study approach is designed for ease and convenience, but is powerful enough to be effective for your most complex and demanding "meals." It is intended to minimize frustration and maximize efficiency. It is hierarchical, so that any of the completed steps will result in information that will be valuable for your rehearsal, even if you are not able to complete them all.

INGREDIENTS:
A bit of time away from distractions to spend with the music
Colored pencils, highlighters, pencils, and pens
Music dictionaries and appropriate language dictionaries
Pitch-pipe
Patience and trust
A good cup of coffee or tea

SERVES:
All choral directors preparing music for all choirs.

Score study can be overwhelming because of the sheer amount of details of the music, even for simple compositions. The notes and rhythms, harmony, meter, dynamics, tonality, diction, composer's indications, melody, form, articulation, translation of the text, and the relationship between the text, the music, and the form, combine to create a list that is seemingly endless and exhausting. In addition, if there are instrumental parts, the conductor must also address additional cues, transpositions, and a variety of clefs. Like a maze, the task seems to have no end, and every time a corner is turned, we just see another path to walk. Even if one had the time to analyze each of these elements, the conductor still would need to internalize and integrate them into a holistic understanding of the piece. As one realizes the amount of effort needed to "know" the music, frustration sets in and conductors often decide to use the learn-as-you-go method. As a result, they make musical mistakes and use rehearsal inefficiently. Perhaps even more significant, conductors miss the personal discovery of the music that can be so rewarding.

The goals for this method are for conductors to: (a) internalize the composition, meaning that the different elements are analyzed and synthesized into a holistic understanding; (b) develop a fondness for score study, to look forward to time alone with the music; and (c) accomplish the specific and identifiable tasks of this method without committing large blocks of time. The key is to focus on a sequential series of elements, avoiding the temptation to be distracted by other musical details and elements. Each step is narrow in scope and can be done quickly. Through analysis and practice, each step results in a greater cognitive and aural understanding of the music.

1. If the text is a foreign language, translate every word. Practice saying the word and thinking the translation of each word. Then practice saying the translation while thinking the text. If you cannot do both, then you do not really know the text.

2. Write in definitions for each musical term. Scan the score for any extra instructions at the bottom of the page, on the inside cover, or in the music at odd places. Avoid being caught thinking you know the gist of the word without really knowing the actual definition.

3. Find and highlight all tempo indications. Practice singing and conducting the changes. Make specific marks, such as new metronome markings, for how much you slow down, exactly where the change occurs, and when a regular tempo is reestablished. Do not allow yourself to make these decisions in the rehearsal by feel. This is how we develop poor recognition of tempo problems. Discipline your mind to know exactly what you want. Always sing at the correct pitch, using a pitch pipe to check your accuracy. Avoid using the piano if possible.

4. Scan the music for any meter changes, and mark and practice as needed. Do not expect to remember the changes and skip the step of marking the music. Practice thinking the text as you conduct the meter. Practice thinking the translation as you conduct the meter.

5. Highlight the development of the melodic material. Search for any movement between the vocal parts. Search the accompaniment or instrumental parts for melodic material as well. Study each part for imitation or hidden motives. Sing the melodic parts while conducting.

6. Highlight (with a different color marker) the rhythmic motives that provide the underlying motor to the music. This might be in the piano (or instrumental parts), or perhaps in harmony choral parts. Alternatively, perhaps the music embeds the basic rhythm in the choral parts.

7. Mark each dynamic indication. Search for instances where the composer is using different dynamic indications in different parts. Sing and conduct the melodic material, careful to put the dynamics into your gesture. Mark any microdynamics that go beyond the composer's instructions that are more general. When it crescendos, exactly how much should the sound increase? Conduct the melody and internalize the pitch with dynamics. If you are up for an audiation challenge, conduct the melody, internalize the pitch with dynamics, and verbally speak the dynamics.

8. Mark the choral parts. Practice singing the different voice parts and making decisions about phrasing, articulations, breaths, and ending consonants. Experiment with different kinds of effects and add marks clearly indicating your preferences. Do not trust your memory for even the smallest detail. Practice singing the microelements while getting these elements into your gesture.

Mark essential cues. Practice cueing while verbally saying the part and looking at where the section would sit. In addition, practice while singing the music and thinking the part while looking at where the section would sit.

10. Find, mark, and explain each accidental. Sing the part to ensure that you understand the melodic or harmonic implication. Scan the music and highlight each difficult interval. Write in the interval above the music, perhaps with solfège.

The purpose of this method is provide a sequential plan for discovering and practicing the musical elements in the music. The power of this approach is that it encourages the conductor to avoid being overwhelmed by the sheer number of details and decisions. In addition, conductors pair intellectual discovery with aural and physical practice to internalize the music. As a result, score study becomes less daunting and more fun, allowing the conductor to become more efficient and dynamic in rehearsals. ➙●